DIARY OF A
MAD PLANNER

DIARY OF A MAD PLANNER

Robert Snetsinger

Winchester Press

Published by Winchester Press
205 East 42nd Street
New York, N.Y. 10017

Printed in the United States of America

WINCHESTER is a Trademark of Olin Corporation
used by Winchester Press, Inc. under authority
and control of the Trademark Proprietor.

Library of Congress Cataloging in Publication Data

Snetsinger, Robert J
    Diary of a mad planner.

    Includes index.
    1. Cities and towns—Planning—United States.
I. Title.
HT167.S6   309.2'12'0973   76-44415
ISBN 0-87691-188-2

Contents

Preface		7
Chapter 1	*My Home Town Makes Good*	9
Chapter 2	*There Is a Season for Building*	35
Chapter 3	*The Snow Came Early*	53
Chapter 4	*People Who Prey Together Stay Together*	69
Chapter 5	*Prime Land Ripe for Development*	85
Chapter 6	*A Lullaby of Turfland*	113
Chapter 7	*It's Raining Cats and Dogs*	135
Chapter 8	*It Is Dangerous to Dream*	159
Index		175

Contents

Preface

It is the purpose of this diary to share personal concerns for the quality of our living space and to encourage good men and women to become involved in planning and local government. Public service is not without its own rewards— camaraderie, a good fight, and even an occasional success (a shopping center with landscaping). For me, the recognition of a need for biological input into urban planning was a major relevance.

This diary takes liberties with time, place, and people, and telescopes many experiences and personalities into composites. One should not look for the communities described on a map or the names of people mentioned in a telephone directory, but look, rather, for a universal accuracy.

Different eyes see events differently, according to experience and perspective. Planning is an emotional activity, because it involves people's rights, money, and dreams. A layman planner is often in the crossfire of developers, home owners, professional planners, solicitors, sewer authorities, and dozens of other groups and individuals. Members of a single planning commission often have strongly opposing views. One's intellect may be in conflict with one's gut responses. Still, all these elements must be focused so that decisions are made. Thus, like planning itself, this diary is paradox.

CHAPTER 1

My Home Town Makes Good

It was a bright Easter morning with a promise of spring in the air. Mother and her daughters-in-law were busy in the kitchen preparing glazed ham with trimmings; her grandchildren were playing in harmony. However, I felt confined by mother's suburban retirement house and decided to stretch my cramped mind and body by a walk out to the old family farmstead.

The distance was but two miles. I used to cover the route at least twice daily all of my youth. (When I was six, I once ran the entire distance; it was a few days after Halloween and I was being followed by a nun whom I believed to be a witch.) Today, as I walked, a kind wind seemed to promise an early meadowlark or the call of a killdeer. The fields were mostly clear of snow, but along the roadside the first beer cans were just starting to bloom through the drifts which were crusted with a winter's accumulation of highway-department cinders.

As I passed the old Robertson farm, there was no flock of sheep to greet me. I recalled one of my old school chums who used to live there, before the land was subdivided. We both owned ponies and traveled all the farm lanes together and knew where the pheasants and the mallards nested.

As I arrived at the family farmstead and approached that farm lane which I have entered ten thousand times or more, I thought of my father, who now lies in a windswept cemetery just a few miles from where he was born. My father had an eye for weather; his alfalfa was rarely rained on. He had an eye for dairy cattle; his holsteins produced not only prize ribbons, but milk in plenty as well. But mostly he had the ability to accept change. One summer when my brother and I were freshly home from agricultural college, we tried to convince father that young chickens should be reared on clean alfalfa pasture, and not in old, disease-infected poultry yards. He listened, but didn't say yes or no. When father left for town on an errand, my brother and I, in the spirit of rebellion, hooked the tractor to the poultry house and moved it to a site our knowledge of poultry science suggested. We expected fireworks when father returned, but he said nothing. The next day, we overheard him telling another farmer to get his young chickens on good alfalfa range, because they develop better, free of worms and disease.

I looked out on the field beyond the barn; the thought flashed through my mind that this is where my brother and I use to spend our Saturdays pulling mustard in the oats, so that father could be proud of his weed-free field when the neighbors passed by on their way to town. A kaleidoscope of a living farm played in my head. A gradual awareness of morning. The banging of milk can covers. The prebreakfast ritual of feeding, milking, cleaning the barns, and driving the cows to pasture. Big-eyed holsteins standing in the creek during the heat of the day. The frenzy of spring, summer, and fall—plowing, planting, cultivating, haying, threshing, fair time, corn picking, the smell of alfalfa drying in the sun, dinner with the threshing crews, and the hum of silo-filling in the fall. Five o-clock. The cows in the pasture lane, their udders caked with mud and teats dripping milk. The big white farmhouse. Watching sunsets from the porch swing. Cold bedrooms in winter. Popcorn and apples around the fireplace when the windows were frosted over. Hot doughnuts fresh from the skillet. Thanksgiving. Christmas. Easter.

I woke from my dreaming. The old barn was still standing, but the haymow doors were missing. There were no cows in the stanchions, no horses in the stalls. Mother had said that sometime this summer the barn would be torn down to make way for an apartment building.

The traffic at the intersection of the new highway and the old route reminded me of how my brother and I used to pull up the surveyor's stakes, in the naive hope that we could reroute the six-lane superhighway to some other place, and thereby save our farm. I looked at the new crop of mustard, thistles, and cockleburs that had sprung up in the field that I use to weed— two gas stations, a motel, a country-fried chicken place, a pizza hut, a drive-in root-beer stand, a factory for making cookie sheets, five prefabricated houses, a ready-mix concrete plant, and a bowling alley. I thought, "God! all that is needed is a mobile home park and an auto junkyard."

Then from somewhere I heard a voice call, "I was once a billowing sea of bluestem, cattails, and slough reeds in the August sun. I was once goldenrod, blazing star, coneflower, and secret spots of purple gentians. I was once a thicket of wild plums, and a fencerow of dust-covered fox grapes. I was once the nest for redwings and bobolinks and the great blue heron. More than a hundred seasons ago your grandfather's father came to live with me. Your father was born in that house sawed of my trees. You and your brothers spent all of your youth with me, except for a natal stay at the city hospital. Your muscle is my meat and grain. Your bones are my milk. Particles of my earth are still beneath your fingernails. I claim you."

Among my father's papers, I once saw Certificate 9023, issued in 1843 and signed by President John Tyler in the sixty-seventh year of the independence of the United States. This certificate assigned ninety-five acres of upland prairie, twenty acres of slough prairie, twenty acres of woodland, and fifteen acres of riparian lake rights to my great-great-grandfather and to his heirs in perpetuity.

When my ancestor arrived to claim Grant 9023, he found it already occupied by whitetail deer, green-winged teal, compass plants, bur oak, and stray Algonquins. With his wife and ten children, my ancestor broke sod, constructed a cabin, killed off wolves, and survived ague and fever. In 1855, my great-grandfather was given care of the farm. His wife managed it for four years while he fought in the American Civil War. Upon his return, they reared a family of five girls, fought chinch bugs, built a new house, and passed the farm on to my grandfather, who had run away from Canada to marry the youngest of the five daughters. My grandfather built new barns, tiled and drained some low areas, and passed the farm on to my father. He struggled through a depression, became a 4-H Club leader, learned new methods of farming, and sent his sons to college. But when the time arrived for my father to pass the farm on to one of his sons, he found it had been stolen. Not by conventional methods, because it was true that my father was paid by the highway department and the developers for his land. Still, he had no choice but to sell. The highway dismembered the fields, the taxes increased because of the highway, the town annexed, and the developers moved in for the killing. I recalled a Saturday in February some years ago when nearly a hundred and fifty farmers and others gathered around two auctioneers and the substance of the old farmstead was sold.

AUCTION

Due to my health, the construction of a highway through my farm, and because my sons are attending college and cannot help me, I am offering my registered herd of Holstein cattle, for sale at my farm residence, located near the intersection of Interstate Highway 21 and Illinois Highway 14, on the old Robertson Road, being at the southwest city limits of Lakegrove. This is one of the best herds of Holsteins in northern Illinois, with a heavy production record and a high test. Calfhood vaccination has been practiced for many years. All females of serviceable age are bred to bulls from the N.I. Breeders Association. In this herd there are many animals that have won ribbons at 4-H fairs. Attend this sale and notice the size, quality, and the good udders these females have. All animals T.B. and Bangs tested. Outstanding Yorkshire gilts and a flock of Southdown sheep are also being sold.

Starting at 1 P.M.   Saturday, February 19, 1965

Thorp Public Auction Service Company
Pete Hank and Peewe Tubbs, Auctioneers

LIVESTOCK – 38 head of registered Holstein Cattle (23 milking, 5 springers, 6 heifers, 4 calves). 15 Yorkshire gilts, bred to farrow March and April. 43 registered Southdown ewes and one 3 year ram, reserve-Champion as lamb ram at Grange County Fair; several ewes are expected to lamb by sale date. 7 rabbits.

MACHINERY AND EQUIPMENT – 63 Farmall Tractor, 1965 3/4 ton Ford pickup truck, 3 bottom plow, mower, corn planter, grain drill, manure spreader, haybailer, rubber-tired wagon, 5 A-frame pig houses, and other equipment and tools, including milking machines and 12 can milk cooler.

FEED – 800 bushels Clinton oats, 500 bushels ear corn, 12 tons of baled alfalfa, 9 tons of baled straw, 18 ft. of silage.

Lunch Trailer on the Grounds

USUAL THORP TERMS

"Now I have $675. Who will give $700 for this outstanding 4-H Club heifer! Going once! Going twice! Gone to number 87 for $675."

By the two hundredth year of independence of the United States, this once-tranquil wilderness, this once-pastoral homestead, this once-modern dairy farm was gone, destroyed. Antoine de Saint-Exupéry's Little Prince said that "once you tame something then you become responsible for it, forever." My family had tamed a homestead. In my mind 4-H Club heifers, pizza huts, hybrid seed corn, neon signs, old tires, and secret patches of purple gentians became all mixed. As I walked back to my mother's house, I thought of Certificate 9023 and how our family had failed; now like the Acadians we must wander from place to place, rootless.

Some months later, my mother's illness brought me back to Lakegrove. The visit was prolonged and depressing. After my daily visit to the hospital, there was little to do but return to my mother's house and wait, or revisit sights of my childhood.

I showed my daughter my old grade school; even though it had been converted to an apartment building, it looked much the same as when I attended grades one through eight. The old Lakegrove elementary was unusual by modern standards; when I attended, it had four large classrooms of which only two were used.

Only thirty to thirty-five students attended; grades one through four were in one room, and five through eight in another. The town library was located in an alcove of the second floor of the school. Each Wednesday from 3:00 to 5:00 P.M. the Lakegrove woman's club made available the two thousand-some volumes. I was a special case, and from the age of ten to twelve was allowed to check out mature books such as *The Scarlet Letter* and *Vanity Fair*, because I had read all the books in the library considered more suitable for my age.

Birthdays in grades one through four were celebrated at school with cake and ice cream. Mothers selected very practical gifts for the children to give to each other. A little girl would open a package and hold up some panties and say, "Look what Jimmy gave me for my birthday." Jimmy would turn red and you would say to yourself, "God, please make what my mother bought something other than that."

Almost every fall, everyone in school was required to furnish the county school principal with a specimen of his writing so that it could be compared with dirty words that had been scrawled on the blackboards of a one-room school that had been vandalized the previous summer; almost everyone wrote the specimen with the left hand—just to play it safe.

The day after the first day of school was Lakegrove Day. The stores and the post office were closed and the residents from Lakegrove went to a picnic ground ten miles away to celebrate. Only the bank was open on this day, and because of this, everyone thought the banker was a snob. Some of the town folks half hoped the banker would be robbed when he was in Lakegrove all by himself.

The town of Lakegrove is located fifty-five miles from the City; early settlers arrived in 1839, shortly after the Algonquins were treatied-out of their lands. At first, Lakegrove was entirely a farming settlement—a couple of stores, a blacksmith shop, a creamery, a school, and a few houses on the shore of Cedar Lake. Shortly after the Civil War, the proximity of the City exerted a slight influence on the community. An ice house was constructed on the south shore of Cedar Lake and a railroad spur ran from the mainline of the Iowa and Northern, so that ice could be transported to the City. During the winter months, many workers came out from the City to Lakegrove to cut and store the ice; they needed a place to stay, and taking in boarders became a way for a great many Lakegrovers to supplement their incomes.

In the 1930s, Lakegrove had a regular population of 350; but during the summers about 100 Northside families from the City moved to lakeside cottages; the husbands came out only on weekends. On Sundays and holidays, and to a lesser degree on Saturdays, several thousand additional Northsiders drove out to Cedar Lake for picnicking, fishing, and to escape the city heat. There were seven major groves around the lake, where for fifty cents the Northsiders were provided access to a beach, picnic tables, slot machines, rowboats, a juke box, and a stand where soda pop, ice cream, sandwiches, and various sundries could be purchased. Also, there were twenty-three taverns around the lake.

Some of the picnics were company affairs, with buses, sound trucks, planned contests, and catered food. Other picnic groups were extended families, descendants of the same grandmother; softball, horseshoes, boccie, swimming, card playing and family squabbles were their main recreation. One of my uncles operated a picnic grove. His was one of the few groves that was open to Jews. Often on Mondays, after he surveyed the smashed tables and garbage cans resulting from a fight between Christian picnickers of differing ethnic background, he would threaten to post his grove "For Jews Only." The Northside Jews all called my relative "Uncle Jim" and blessed him with Kosher corned beef, pickles, and money. Despite these summer people, Lakegrove remained rural.

The three major churches in the community were German Reformed, German Lutheran, and German Catholic. Before 1917 most of the farmers spoke only German; during World War I, nobody spoke it; by 1919 all the farmers spoke English with a German accent. By the next war, only a few old farmers knew German. Still everyone called friends even of long standing Mr. and Mrs. and not by their first names; the farmers continued to paint barns red and to be intolerant of thistles.

The important time of day in Lakegrove was 8:00 A.M. when the farmers hauled their milk to a central pickup point. While the hired man, the wife, or the children cleaned the barn and finished the morning chores, the farmers talked about prices, crops, and the war. At the general store they bought groceries, joked, snitched cookies, and played games with dart boards or popguns on display for Christmas; usually at least one child in every family got a worn-out dart board or a popgun with a weak spring on Christmas morning. By 9:00, the farmers arrived home with their empty milk cans and Lakegrove "snoozed," until awakened by the fire whistle that sounded noon and released the high schoolers who rendezvoused at Brown's Place until 12:45; again at 3:30, the students enlivened the center of town.

When you were little, the fireman's carnival was a big deal. The little kids always hung around and watched the merry-go-round, the ferris wheel, various rides, and stands being assembled; sometimes a roustabout would ask the biggest kid "where is the cat house,Sonny?" Nobody knew what a cat house was. On the Fourth of July all the kids spent their money on firecrackers, skyrockets, and Roman candles. When you were in high school, basketball was big; on Tuesday and Friday evenings during the season everybody went to home or away games. After you graduated from high school you became a barber or gas-station attendant, worked in the store, or helped your father on the farm. I was different; I went away to the university. Eight years later when I was in graduate school and I came home to visit my parents, people would stop me and ask, "how come you're still in college?"

Lakegrove had changed since I was a kid. Just before World War II, a few wealthy families had bought farms; they remodeled the farmhouses, rented the farmland to adjoining farmers, commuted to the City to work and shop, but in general adapted to Lakegrove's ways. After World War II, a second wave of wealthy newcomers bought up dairy farms and constructed white fences to contain their saddle horses; their intrusion drastically inflated farmland prices, causing many Lakegrove farmers to sell out and purchase farms in central Wisconsin. Starting in the mid-1950s, a few local subdividers and developers started satellite communities around Lakegrove; the influx of new residents caused crowded schools, above ground sewage, and soaring taxes. In the mid-1960s larger developers moved in and started projects of two hundred to four hundred homes and two shopping centers. Then, in the 1970s, several factories moved from the City to Lakegrove.

The school districts were consolidated in 1956; all the one- and two-room schools were combined, and the children bused to a central school; then, as the community continued to grow, schools split again. The Cedar Lake Elementary School now has 894 and the Mabel Fox Elementary School has 653 students. The Lakegrove Junior High has 773 and the Lakegrove Senior High has 807 students. When I was in first grade, there were 3 in my class; my high school graduating class of 32 was the largest in the history of the school; that was twenty-three years ago. A year ago, a first cousin graduated from high school in a class of 284. My second cousin is in a "new," ungraded, open elementary classroom; it has 135 students with 2 teachers and 2 teacher's aids.

Our family doctor when I was a young boy was Dr. Graver; he had twinkling eyes and a belly like Saint Nick's; he made house calls and treated people rather than diseases. When my mother gave birth to my youngest brother during Depression times, my father asked, "How much if I pay cash?" Dr. Graver said, "OK, $20.00 off for cash." There is a new breed of doctors in Lakegrove. They spend most of their time in operating rooms. Their patients sit like zombies in the waiting rooms of their "clinics." A bitchy receptionist informs the incoming zombies that "the doctor is operating" and that they "will just have to wait." A certain number of the zombies are processed by the nurses. When the doctor arrives, he dispenses pills and charisma. Eventually the smart people in Lakegrove go to a chiropractor and the intelligent ones don't get sick and the wealthy ones go to specialists in the City. The zombies wait.

As I discovered the "new" Lakegrove, it struck me that local politics had changed. My father, grandfather, and great-grandfather had all served on the village board of Lakegrove; the family homestead was just within the village limits. I recall how directly the village problems were solved. When my father was on the board, the town marshal got drunk one night and drove the new police car part way across Cedar

Lake. The next day the village board met and fired the old marshal and hired a new one. In the old days the town was run by the old families and the merchants. Now it is run by the real-estate people and the undertakers. The land developers get whatever they want and the older residents in the community get the runaround, because they do not understand the new red tape. The village board, the planning commission, and the zoning board all agree that new factories and new homes increase the tax base and therefore are good.

In 1847, my great-grandfather paid $10.47 in school taxes on 150 acres; my mother's school taxes last year were $847.35 on her 75-by-150 foot lot and six-room retirement house. Each year taxes increase and the quality of life in Lakegrove deteriorates for those that were born there and those that have moved there.

Yet Lakegrove is getting bigger and better, according to the wording on the signs that welcome you. Over the years I carefully read the three weekly Lakegrove newspapers that my mother forwarded to me when something was happening. The chamber of commerce was always on the make for new industry. The members established an industrial park and worked out tax advantages for anyone who sniffed at moving to Lakegrove. I recall reading of the great day when the mayor and the chamber announced that General Paint Industries was to establish a factory across from the Lakegrove Senior High School. Also, I recall a not-so-great day when the village board discovered that, due to an error in the final contract specifications, their new sewage plant was designed to handle a population of 2,000 instead of 20,000. The life and times of my hometown via the local newspapers has been a bittersweet soapbox opera. As I read the Lakegrove *Freepress* last night, I didn't know if I should laugh or cry. The main story was:

General Paint Bankruptcy Petition Filed

LAKEGROVE – A bankruptcy petition is expected to be filed in Federal District Court Thursday by General Paint Industries, Inc. Harlow Waters, Company president, Wednesday announced his intention to file for bankruptcy. A check at the Federal Court at the State Capitol did, however, show that bankruptcy actions had not been filed as of presstime today.

Waters declined to further comment on whether bankruptcy was declared, and if so in what court. In

another development, General Paint company officials were served with papers demanding payment
of $2,731,415 owed to the Exchange National Bank.
The writ, filed in Grange County, directs that a levy
be placed on the General Paint property in Lakegrove. John Beppler, attorney for the Exchange National Bank, said the $2.7 million was part of capital
advanced to General Paint by the bank. In addition
to the 2.7 million, the writ asks payment of $123,472
in attorney's fees and $19,875 in interest. The com-
pany also faces lawsuits for $94,000 from the Lake-
grove Industrial Improvement Association, and
$52,121 from Harry Richmond of Lakegrove,
former president of General Paint.

The bankruptcy action places the jobs of 33 administration employees and 230 production employees in jeopardy. The company came to Lakegrove in 1969 and is located in the Lakegrove Industrial Park.

As I drove into the City from Lakegrove the
next day, I made a special detour so as to pass
the original site of the General Paint company
at Western and Lincoln avenues, on the near
Northside. I noted black children playing in a
rundown schoolyard, just across the street from
the first General Paint factory. I got out of my
car and walked down an alley that separated
the backyards of a nearby block of row houses.

In the middle of the block, the city sanitation department was making its rounds. I walked behind the garbage truck for two blocks, noting that about half of the litter was left in the alley. I asked one of the city workers why all the materials were not picked up. He explained that they were required to remove only those materials that are placed in the type of container prescribed by city regulations. All other materials must be left to be picked up by a different crew on a monthly basis. I noted two rats scurry away from a pile of garbage; this indicated that things must get pretty lively in that alley with the coming of night.

Just as I was getting ready to go back to my car, I was stopped by someone who appeared to be a white landlord type. I was wearing a suit and he must have thought I was some kind of City inspector. "You got a real problem here," he said.

This City always had big problems. Many of my impressions of the City were formed before I was six. An abandoned car left on the roadside by our farm was the depository for a minor city hood who had met with debris from a submachine gun. Also, Babyface Nelson got it, but six miles down the road from my home. Of course, Grange County was not much better than the City; its main difference was that it was Republican while the City was Democratic. The Grange County slot-machine wars were always lively. One Sunday, when I was about twelve, the word got out that a rival gang was to invade Lakegrove and destroy all the machines. The local picnic grove and tavern owners brought about fifty slot machines to our farm to hide; I helped one of my relatives bury them beneath a mound of ear corn until things cooled off. Some years later, a Democratic governor sent half the state police into Grange County on a slot-machine raid. The police blocked off a six-lane highway and collected a small mountain of machines.

However, my first impressions of the City were not of gang wars and booze barons. I made trips with relatives and friends to the zoo, to the Ringling Brothers Circus, to baseball games, to livestock shows, and the stockyards when we shipped a load of pigs. The stench of the buses, bums sleeping beneath newspaper coverlets, black children expectorating on my grandfather's car, and hot dogs with onions, pickles, tomatoes, and mustard that burnt your guts all the way home from the baseball game, stand out. When I returned from these trips, my bladder and bowels were always extended to the bursting point; my mother discouraged the use of public toilets because of fearful, unmentionable diseases that could be contacted from toilet seats.

Still, somehow, like Dick Whittington, I thought the City's streets were paved with gold. The tall towers, the great homes on the Gold Coast, and the stores offered luxuries compared with Lakegrove's water tower, milk factory, drug store, drygoods store, three general stores, post office, and twenty-three taverns.

The city girls who summered at the various cottages around Cedar Lake contributed to my knowledge of urban life. The little ones played "one-two-three-o-leary-o" on the tiny bits of sidewalk that Lakegrove afforded. The city children feared the wilder, rougher "redwing" and "red rover" of their rural contemporaries. The older city girls somehow were more interesting than the rural girls; this despite the city girl's ignorance of the origin of horse apples and their urge to slide down straw stacks—a serious breach of rural ethics.

During high school, it wasn't really the girls

that drew me to the City, but the plays, museums, book stores, and even professional baseball games. These continued to attract me to the City while I was attending college. However, involvement in the State Young Democratic Organization took me to conventions, state meetings, and allowed me to meet candidates for state and local office. The wishes of the Big Mayor were followed by most of those Y-Ds playing politics; they got their rewards when they became young City lawyers. The City machine brought brothelites to State Young Democrat conventions to render service; many elections were lost between one and four A.M. One whore was even elected Third Vice-President of the National Young Democrats. However, I also met Young Turks intent on reform. Some got bent over the years, but others continued to tilt against the Big Mayor's windmill machine.

The City used to be held together by ethnic glue. There were Polish neighborhoods, Italian neighborhoods, Irish neighborhoods, black neighborhoods, Greek neighborhoods, Lithuanian neighborhoods, Bohemian neighborhoods, and others. These neighborhoods were small towns with their own local tavern, bakery, movie house, drugstore, butcher shop, police station, baseball field, pool hall, whore, drunk, barber shop, main street, gossip, and politics. Every four blocks on the major street was downtown. No one had to go farther to find his wants. If he did, he was just asking for trouble—the street gang might get him. Inter-neighborhood baseball was often a jarring contact sport. The borders of a neighborhood often had a gray area where outsiders were moving in; here fights often occurred. Outsiders soon learned to stay away from "Jewtown" or to refuse to join in a rock festival at "Polock Park." It is nice to sentimentalize blindly about how great the old City was. But was it so great when mobsters controlled City Hall and black children were stoned to death for swimming on those beaches "belonging" to white neighbor "hoods"?

My second city was always Amsterdam. However, my Amsterdam was that of *Hans Brinker or the Silver Skates*. The churches, chimneys, canals, dogcarts, windmills, sweeping, mopping, scrubbing, tulips, and storks, all were as real to me as John Dillinger. From a

planning tour I once took of Amsterdam, I remember the Dutch word *gezelligheid*, which
describes the ability of people to live together
in a community with compassion, tolerance,
variety, and security—an agreement to coexist.
This spirit is what makes Amsterdam a great
city.

As I reviewed my recent encounters with my
"new" hometown and the City's Northside, I
recalled no *gezelligheid*. I gave up my inspec-
tion around the birthplace of the General Paint
company, so that I could get to my in-laws in
time for dinner. But first I had to pick up a City
paper for my father-in-law. As I read the headlines, I was not surprised to see an account of a
brutal rape on the City's Northside.

CHAPTER 2

There Is a Season for Building

EDITORIAL

For everything there is a season, and a time for every matter under heaven:

A time to design highways and a time for surveying for highways;

A time to review plans and a time for hearings;

A time for questions and a time to refrain from questioning;

A time for saving old homesteads and a time to pour concrete;

The time is at hand to start construction of the middle section of the bypass.

All the facts have been gathered, all the hearings have been held.

All the protests have been registered.

All the arguments in favor of construction have been presented.

The longer we wait, the longer we will waste two sections of a road to nowhere.

The longer we wait, the more we will suffer the crush of inadequate roads.

The longer we wait, the greater will be the construction costs.

The editorial in this morning's paper continued with a story of a struggle of nearly ten years by one community over a highway corridor. It concluded with: "Finishing the bypass will help us to catch up with the rest of the world. It is essential for the economic growth of our community, whether or not we like it."

I had to admit that today's editorial has a nice ring, even if it is a bit funerary. However, the newly formed citizen's association is not about to accept the latest highway corridor. Lunch today is yet another planning meeting concerned with highways. I have been on my township and regional planning commissions both for ten years, and my lunches during this period have consisted of a heavy diet of relocations, environmental impact studies, petitions from citizen's groups, locations of shopping center ingresses and egresses, and impending disasters to duck ponds and other natural beauties. One has to admire the efficiency and dedication of the State transportation department. Modern technology has speeded the normal five-hundred-year waiting period traditionally observed by phoenixes. Once defeated, highway interchanges arise from the ashes of their blueprints within months of their deaths.

Today's meeting is a special work session in order to try to gain additional concessions from the State transportation department. Three months ago, the various local planning commissions, the regional planning commission, the council of local governments, and most of the citizenry were willing to accept the sketch plan of the proposed highway corridor. However, the final design suggests that the highway people weren't quite forthright in their earlier statements. It appears that they still intend to make the local bypass part of the Intermountain Thruway. This is indicated by their interchange design. The less-than-favorable reception that the corridor hearing for the Intermountain Thruway got last Monday is part of a increasing public pressure against bringing this route up our valley, rather than the earlier proposed route in the next valley west.

Because I am chairman of the regional planning commission, I am an exofficio member of the council on local government's transportation committee. Since planning commissions in our state are purely advisory and exofficio members have similar potency, I am doubly detoothed. The supervisors of the four townships and the councilmen from borough have the final word at this stage of the negotiations. Today's subcommittee will report back to the full local government council.

Since many of the members of the committee have to get back to their jobs by 1:30, the regional planning director explains the purpose of the meeting and outlines the problems and possible alternatives right at the start of the luncheon of burgers and coffee.

The first to speak is Warren T. Maxwell, a councilman from the borough. He has been on the borough council for sixteen years and owns five service stations. "To hell with the new citizen's group anyway! We've wasted enough time arguing over the location of the bypass. We were elected to make decisions and not to listen to crybaby groups with crackpot ideas! So what if the highway is to be located on an elevated dike across the valley? If nature made the dike, the goddamn environmentalists would call it a terminal moraine and think it the most beautiful natural feature in the region. Let those bastards in the citizen's association bring on their injunction. Let the courts settle this thing, once and for all. We've accommodated and accommodated. Hell, let's get this highway built."

This starter by the gas station owner brought the meeting alive. The supervisor from Russell Township choked on his burger. His great-grandfather was one of the earliest settlers in the county. He runs a dairy farm that has been in his family for three generations. "I'm not against highways," the dairy farmer said, "but I think that the location of the Intermountain Thruway needs to be settled before we approve this middle section of the bypass. We are putting the cart before the horse; how can we approve the bypass interchange without some assurance that we don't get the Intermountain Thruway to boot? I'm against the thruway, because it will destroy thirty-five good farms in Russell Township. The farms in my township are long and narrow. If the thruway goes down our valley, it will make it impossible to farm in Russell Township. Most of the farmers have at least $100,000 invested in buildings, equipment, and livestock. When my father started farming there were more than a thousand farms in the county. Now there are fewer than three hundred. We need every farm we can save if we are to feed our country." Two others and I applauded.

However, Jack Shore, the other borough councilman wasn't happy. He owns two motels and a construction company. "The supervisor from Russell Township neglected to state that his farm is likely to be affected. I think that we gotta get down to the real issue. God knows that with all the time I spend in these meetings, my office staff rarely sees me. The real issue is the location of the interchange." The motel councilman continued, "We gotta recognize that for a community to stay alive, it must grow. We must increase new business so we can have a larger tax base. We must have highways so that new business will want to establish in our community. Each day that we put off construction of this highway, it is costing us money."

I asked the motel councilman: "If highway construction increases land value, because it places demands about the interchange for motels, gas stations, and restaurants, and since the general public paid for the highway construction, why not place an interchange tax on those businesses located at the interchange?"

He asked me: "Are you some kind of communist?" This got a twitter from two or three committee members.

Tom Emory, who is the executive secretary of the chamber of commerce, was recognized and in turn briefly introduced Dr. James Lewis, who had just completed a study for the Intermountain Thruway Economic Development Council on the impact of the proposed thruway on the county. Dr. Lewis is on the staff at Southern University, where he is a statistician in their college of engineering. He explained that he would be releasing a full report this evening at the courthouse to the Development Council and that he appreciated an opportunity to briefly explain his study to us. He said that "when completed the thruway and bypass would bring $18.9 million in travel sales to the county. Every person who drives the thruway or interstate generates $2.36 for the local economy for some 358 firms that employ 3,116 persons." Lewis claimed that by 1984, the county's travel trade would increase to an 11.9 percent from the present 7.1 percent.

I could see that Michael Philipps, from the Laurel Mountain Conservancy Club, was getting upset. He yelled, "What kind of packed meeting is this? Why do we have to listen to this crap from a pondering ass of a professor who can be bought for a few pieces of silver? Why doesn't Professor Lewis stay at home and teach his classes?" The civil engineer councilman took the floor and moved "that Philipps be instructed to shut up or be removed from the meeting since only the citizen's association had been invited to this meeting."

Grant Horner, the regional engineer for the State transportation department, was recognized. He explained that the proposed highway "would harmonize with the aesthetics and the ecological balance of the region" and how a "lovely white carpet of concrete would carry friends and visitors to the beautiful mountains of our region." I thought to myself, "How full of crap can you get?" Everytime I hear Horner speak I get an upset stomach. He seems to believe that he is building highways on the site God intended for them to be located, and that no one in their right mind should question the veracity of a highway engineer. The only kid that I know who grew up to be a highway engineer used to kick down everybody else's sand castles when he was four. However, the power to condemn and take away other people's property and bulldoze it to a prescribed mold does not promote humility toward nature or your fellow man, and one is hard pressed to find any public evidence of humility and concern for environmental quality in Grant Horner.

The president of the citizen's association, Nancy Thurston, was then recognized. She thanked the regional planner and the committee for an opportunity to present the association's position. She cited a recent study that suggested local vehicle trips accounted for 90 percent of the traffic, while intracity trips were about 10 percent, considerably down from sixteen years ago. This, she claimed, was because of improved connections to the east-west interstate. She also observed that "the proposed highway crossed the major well fields for the region, and that the highway department had not considered the potential effect of road construction on the purity of the water." She asked why no formal agreement had been obtained relevant to replacement of parklands to be taken by the highway right-of-way? How could the people who live to the north of the bypass use Clearfield Park? The only way was to cross the highway at an interchange two miles away and then walk or drive back. Why not a pedestrian underpass opposite the park? Nancy questioned spending twenty to thirty million dollars on a road that would "have little beneficial effect on local traffic problems and cause so much harm to natural features." She concluded that "the citizen's association still planned to hire a lawyer to fight the transportation department unless a better solution can be found."

As the gas station councilman started to speak for the second time, my mind began to wander. The meeting room was transformed into a courtroom. There was a jury, lawyers, and a judge, and all the seats in the courtroom were filled. The bailiff was just announcing a case. "Hear ye! Hear ye! The Citizen's Association versus the Automobile, Judge Carroll Tressler presiding." The Blue Sedan was accused of murdering 10,000 pedestrians in only one year. One witness claimed that the Sedan came from a family of murderers and that the Sedan and its kin had killed 300,000 men, women, and children during the past ten years. The Judge ruled this statement out of order. A wildlife expert from Virginia testified that he had observed the Sedan kill 95 animals over a stretch of six miles. Included in his list were 31 rabbits, 24 skunks, 15 opossum, 7 foxes, 4 groundhogs, 2 squirrels, 2 raccoons, 1 mink, 1 muskrat, 3 quail, and 5 undetermined birds. A game protector from Pennsylvania stated the Sedan killed 25,000 deer in the previous year. The lawyer for the Sedan argued that the Sedan was attempting to make driving more comfortable by lining the roads with fur. A citizen who had been involved in Earthday activities claimed that he and a group of others had picked up some 20,000 bottles and cans plus other trash along a two mile stretch of a narrow country road, all dumped there by the

Sedan. He also stated that it would cost at least five billion dollars annually to clean up all the litter along U.S. highways. An expert on city planning claimed that the Sedan was using between 40 and 70 percent of the space in our major cities, leaving little room for human activities. The attorney for the citizen's association continued to call experts on air pollution, mass transportation, aesthetics, and on city planning, all of whom presented testimony unfavorable to the Sedan. Very few objections were raised as to the truth of their testimony; however, the Judge ruled that such testimony was out of order and not relevant. The attorney for the citizen's association completed his case against the Sedan with an elegant and inflammatory closing statement.

After a short recess, the attorney for the Sedan said, "Judge Tressler, I have only one witness to call." A middle-aged gas pump took his seat in the witness box. The pump simply said, "I have known the Sedan for all of his life. He is an important member of our community and drives over a trillion miles in his work each year. He buys more than 100 billion gallons of gasoline from me each year and pays hard cash. He pays more state and federal taxes than anyone else and employs more than 13 million people." The defense attorney quickly described what the world would be like without the Sedan; he used words like public transportation, walking, and biking and the jury gasped; and he then quickly closed his case. The jury filed out, but returned within seven minutes and delivered a verdict of "not guilty." Someone next to me nudged me and I returned to hear the supervisor from Freeport Township complain that "accord on the location had been reached six months ago and now some people have failed to live up to their commitments." It was past 1:15; obviously nothing will be settled today. The chairman appointed a subcommittee of three to meet with the citizen's association before the meeting next week of the whole committee.

I headed back to my office. At the first stop light, I looked at my watch and recorded an interval of fifty seconds for the "Don't Walk" light. The "Walk" time was ten seconds. It took me eight seconds to cross the intersection; the cars did it in four. During the time I was allowed to walk, cars were allowed to make left turns into my crossover. By rough calculation, I figured I had about one eighth the rights of a car. This train of thought started me comparing benches versus parking lots, rest rooms for motorists versus rest rooms for pedestrians, and directional signs for motorists versus signs for walkers; always the pedestrian came out the loser. I thought, "Well at least I am better off than the chickens in Quitman, Georgia." One of the fillers in last Sunday's paper reported that in Quitman, a new ordinance made it unlawful for chickens to cross the road. In most places, when chickens try to cross the road, they are as dead as that old joke about why it is that chickens cross roads.

I crossed the next street the regular way instead of using the underpass. A few years ago, when four students were seriously injured and one killed crossing this intersection, the university spent nearly $150,000 constructing an underpass. To avoid crossing a street that is thirty-three feet wide, it is necessary to go down a flight of twenty-three steps then pass down a grotto a hundred feet in length and then up another twenty-three steps. Anyone who has observed students create cowpaths all over the campus just to save a few steps in passage between classes could have forecast the failure of the underpass. It is so little used that even deviates and muggers avoid it. The underpass is used only by pornographers and an art class for mural painting every spring. Every time I use the damn tunnel, I say to myself, "Why didn't they lower the road and let the people walk over?" One of the pornographers had written on the grotto wall, "There is life after the womb." This, and the avoidance of the underpass by students, suggests that my friend in psychology who always says, "we all want to go back to the womb anyway," doesn't know what he is talking about.

The other side of my question to the motel councilman is still bugging my mind. Does the transportation department rightfully use its power of eminent domain? I know of two neighboring farms, one now on one side of an interstate and one on the other. Each own about thirty severed acres on the wrong side of the road. Neither farmer can effectively till or pasture these fields; however, if the transportation department had taken both severed acreages and then arbitrated an exchange between the farmers, both farm operations would have benefited. Anytime two pieces of farm land are severed, the flexibility of the farm operation is reduced. This seems to be just one of the factors that is not paid for by the transportation department when it takes land. The loss of ten to fifteen acres taken for highway construction is often just enough to make many family-type farms unprofitable; this means the eventual abandonment of barns and other farm buildings—a loss of capital. Again, this is not covered by payments to the farmer. The family farmer and the small landholder are very much exploited by cars. Expressways have smashed many stable urban neighborhoods, and destroyed many businesses; urbanites are forced to become suburbanites; now they must substitute for a friendly beer at the neighborhood bar, a weekly romp with the power mower in suburbia. The cars have it better; they no longer spend their nights on the street.

Just yesterday, the supervisors in Russell Township approved their second motorcycle track. Mr. Gary Trueblood, who owns the Freewheeling Cycle Shop, claimed that since the township had already allowed his competitor a track, they must allow him one also. The main purpose of the track is to promote Kamikaze motorcycles; his competition, who already has a motorcycle track, is doing well selling Hairy Davisons to sexagenarian teen-agers, leatherjacketeers, and others who rec-reate by going around and around a barren field of grass. Of course here and there the landscape is broken by signs for ESP motor oil.

When I was a small child I used to amuse myself by spending hours behind the steering wheel of an old Ford truck going "Brun! Brun!" and delivering cans of milk to town and per-forming other imaginary errands. When I was a boy, I could recognize a 1948 DeSoto or a 1949 Mercury with the best of them. The person who could recognize the first of the current year's vintage cars and cite all of their special features was looked up to by all his grade-school friends. Like other Americans we were learning to revere the automobile.

It often strikes me, when I drive past a com-munity with crippled, nonfunctional cars stored in front yards, that Americans worship dead cars instead of God! In the beginning there were headlights and in the end taillights.

Each year 50,000 lives are offered on the altar of the highway. This far exceeds the efforts of any other primitive peoples to meet their lust for blood. Might not the national system of interstate and defense highways be the true cathedral of America?

CHAPTER 3

The Snow Came Early

"Here is a land of woods, water, quiet mountains, and clear skies. Here is a community with all the conveniences and comforts of urban life, yet providing a truly idyllic way to live. Here in a majestic panorama of changing seasons is a well-planned, protected, and secluded city.

"Year around, you and your family can live the fun life of fishing, waterskiing, boating, swimming, golf, tennis, hiking, horseback riding, ice-skating, and skiing. Join the exclusive social set at the magnificent Keystone Lake Country Club. The nicest thing of all is that Keystone City is whatever you want it to be. Breathe pure, invigorating mountain air. Have an abundant private life admidst wealth of natural beauty. Live where everyday is a glorious exhilarating experience.

"To visit Keystone City, take Interstate 77 to Exit 31, then take Route 155 4.7 miles south until you reach the new Keystone entrance. Here you will be greeted by a charming Keystone hostess. She will introduce you to the scenic delights of Keystone's jewel-blue lake and emerald-green forest. She will open the Olympic-sized swimming pool and the eighteen-hole golf course to your pleasure. If you call and make advance arrangements, we will show you our choice homesites and be your host for dining at the Keystone Lake Country Club. There is no cost to you. There will be no high-pressure sales pitch. We want you to see Keystone City and leisurely make up your own mind."

The founders of Keystone City launched their project five years ago with a fanfare of banquets for local officials, full-page features in the regional newspapers, and by paying the travel expenses of the local high-school marching band to the Orange Bowl Parade. The Keystone Township planning commission hastily added a planned community district amendment to their zoning ordinance. The supervisors anticipated handsome increases in tax revenues. The chamber of commerce started a campaign to increase the size of the local airport so that prospective Keystone clients could be flown in from all over the East.

Two of my friends took advantage of a free weekend visit to Keystone City about a year ago. Twenty couples from New England boarded a Keystone company jet at Boston. They were served breakfast en route and arrived at "Keystone Airfield" two hours later. A few minutes were allowed to freshen up and then the group was ushered into the conference center for a seminar on Keystone City. A young man in an expensive suit introduced himself as an assistant planner in charge of long-range planning and open-space design. "At present," the young man explained, "the parks and natural areas are administered by the Keystone Development Corporation, but as more and more of the sites are sold and built upon, then a home owner's association will gradually gain control. Thus each family truly owns Keystone City with all its natural wealth." The planner, by means of multicolored maps and a scaled model for the year 2000, glowingly described Keystone's future growth. Then each couple

was taken by a Keystone hostess to see the site
of the new ultramodern elementary school, the
first phase of the partially completed shopping
center, the community church which will have
three Sunday services for different denomina-
tions, the site of the proposed teenage
clubhouse, the swimming pool, the tennis
courts, the eighteen-hole championship golf
course, and the wooded home sites overlooking
Keystone Lake and within convenient walking
distance of school site, shopping, and recreation. The couples were rushed back to the
conference center where they were served free
cocktails. Shortly, a busy, talkative sales man-
ager, Rudy Joly, breezed across the thickly car-
peted conference room and introduced himself
to the twenty couples. Soon it was, "Bob and
Gladys, let me freshen your drinks" or "Dave
and Alice, did you get a chance to see that lot
on Rising Sun Lane?" or "Harry and Jeannie,
we sold a lot to another couple from Bridgeport
just last week." After each couple had received
at least their second drink, Rudy asked for the
group's attention and lead them into a side
room which was muralized with scenes of
mountains, lakes, and country villages. Joly

explained that "$2050 invested three years ear-lier would now be worth $3750." Joly asked, "How many of you would like to make $500 in one year?" He then rapidly wrote figures on a green chalkboard that proved $2350 invested in a lot today would be worth $2850 next year. He then explained how $200 down and $30 per month would net them $500 in one year. During this explanation, an assistant to Joly rushed into the room and explained in a loud whisper that an investment company in St. Louis, Missouri, wanted to purchase 200 lots the next day. Joly told the twenty couples that he could only keep the lot prices at $2350 until banquet time that evening. My friends escaped, visited me, and paid their own fare back to Boston.

"Picture yourself," says an ad in tonight's paper, "strolling with your handsome dog at your side in a field of wildflowers spread out like a gypsy's colored skirt. Queen Anne's lace, black-eyed Susan, and golden heads of timothy bobbing in the breeze. Then you enter a wooded glade and the chipmunks and squirrels scamper away with their cheeks filled with acorns from the rich forest of oak. You can chat with a neighbor who is on a bird-watching hike and then return to your new bilevel, stylish wood and stone, comfortable, carefree, three-bedroom rancher; pass through the traditional courtyard and enter the distinctive Colonial door into your large living room with its stone fireplace and magnificent view of Mount Pinetop; turn left into the attractive dining room (plenty of room for your natural-wood Colonial dining-room set). Next stop is the kitchen with a Legstrong floor so beautiful it will make you believe in magic carpets again. This kitchen is a joyful place to work and is fit for any President and his First Lady. There are three bedrooms located on a level removed from the rest of the home, two baths, and many other wonderful features. Call us, we have the key to your dream."

I watched that dream being built. The flowery gypsy's skirt was a neglected, weedy field. The backfill around the foundation of the comfortable rancher is a mixture of construction trash and logs and branches from the destruction of the on-site trees—a termite heaven. The trim and siding hide all sins.

The report of the President's Commission on Population Growth predicts that University

City, the home of the State University, will be a major metropolitan area by the year 2000. The commission's research staff described the growth pattern of University City as similar to that of 120 other major-cities-to-be. Since big cities and their surrounding megalopolises are considered to be overpopulated already, the commission's recommendation is to try to head off further migrations from farms or small towns to major cities by further facilitating the growth of the 121 medium-sized cities. The commission estimated that some sixty-five million people will move to these new locales or will have their present town incorporated into these growth centers. The same research paper notes also that if this policy is not implemented and backed by government programs, there will be a much faster decline of non-metropolitan places than is now going on.

When the carefully guarded list of 121 growth centers was released last month, it was learned that the federal government had been planning this program for over three years. There was an immediate furor raised by the citizens of University City. "What the hell are those Washington people trying to do? Don't

we have any say so about our own town?" The
county planning commission wrote letters to
Washington and the local citizen's action
league wrote letters to the newspaper. No re-
plies came from Washington and everyone
concluded that the whole thing was another
Washington hoax.

My Sunday paper gave an account of Dr.
William Burkhard, who is to give a lecture "Urban Pollution and its Solution" at the State
University. Dr. Burkhard won international
acclaim for his work on electromagnetic fields.
Currently Burkhard is the idol of the campus
speaking circuit, discussing environmental
problems. He claims that most of New Jersey's
shoreline area, a considerable portion of New
York City, and sizeable sections of the New
England coastal plain will be inundated by a
devastating flood caused by poor ecological
planning. In a recent book, *Living Within Nature*, Burkhard, according to his reviewer,
"proposes concrete ecological solutions for sol-
ving urban problems with a stimulating concept of 'least social cost'—a system based on
scientific principles that have the virtue of considering the needs of everyone." The article in

the Sunday paper, stated that *Living Within Nature* "describes an America saved from ecological disaster by the formidable weapons of ecology against the forces of ignorance, of unconscionable profit, and of exploitation." I went to the lecture and all that I learned was "planned growth is more desirable than uncontrolled growth" and that Burkhard is a chain smoker. I left the lecture early.

The student paper the next morning gave a glowing account of Burkhard's lecture. It seems that the "total mass of humanity now on earth weighs 200 million tons or 1/10,000th of the mass of all animal life. When mankind increases its number 10,000-fold, then *Homo sapiens* will be, per force, the only animal species alive on earth. It will be a world without elephants or lions, without cats or guinea pigs, without fish or lobsters, without worms or bugs. The whole world will be one Pruitt-Igoe. High-rise apartments will spread across all the mountains, across the Sahara Desert, across the Antarctic, across all the oceans. The roofs of all the buildings will be algae farms and the cellars will be mushroom caves. The heat from the people will melt the polar icecaps. Burkhard asked the question, "What would happen if the algae got tired?" Somehow I missed the boat by leaving early.

This morning's mail included an environmental report from the Santa Rubens Oil Company. It described their new $7 million offshore platform ten miles out in the Santa Rubens Channel.

"The gulls cry through the morning mists. Slowly the sun begins driving the fog out to sea. Then barely visible, silhouetted against the gray morning sky, emerges a blue-painted platform which blends with the churning channel waters; it looks like a ship sailing through the channel in the distance. It's Santa Rubens' new, fail-safe, antipollution oil-directing platform which is equipped with the most advanced engineering features devised by petroleum engineering, which is one of the most advanced fields of engineering today.

"The skills exhibited by the men who work on this flotation cell are those of the best in the oil business. Take Bob Whitmore, senior project engineer, he's an easygoing, smiling individual. But on the job, he's strictly business, a no-nonsense professional. Moreover, his drilling crews and supervisors have been thoroughly trained in handling safety equipment and in checking equipment regularly to provide up-to-the minute maintenance.

"The most pressing question offshore oilmen are asked these days is 'What are the chances of a blowout occurring again?' 'Hardly any,' says Bob Whitmore. 'We have taken every precaution to prevent such a thing from happening. These new platforms are designed to withstand wind, wave, and earthquake conditions at the drilling sites. If anything goes wrong and isn't corrected immediately, the entire platform shuts down automatically, with all valves and vessels closing shut, rather than open.' To such men as Bob Whitmore, the stern challenge of taking every precaution is a double-edged task. But offshore oilmen are used to risks and challenges. They are also men who have a deep concern for the environment. The objective of Bob Whitmore and others like him is to meet the nation's increasing demands for petroleum products, and, at the same time, take every precaution to protect the environment." I only hope that good old Bob doesn't have to eat oily seagull again.

"West Aaron is going to court," tonight's paper reported. Richard Winslow, attorney for the town, received the unanimous support of fifty-five townspeople to fight a Commonwealth Environmental Agency order for the construction of a sewage collection and treatment system that would cost $2.5 million, more than seven times the assessed value of all real estate in the borough.

"This is not just a case of financial hardship," said Winslow. "This is an impossible and ridiculous outrage. There are only 316 townspeople, and most of them are retired and living on pensions. About a year ago, the CEA ordered West Aaron to draw up plans for a sanitary sewer system and treatment facility. The town council then turned the order over to an engineering firm, which prescribed the $2.5 million project. Last week the Environmental Hearing Board turned down West Aaron's appeal."

Saying he would file the court appeal next week, Winslow "claimed that coming up with the $35,000 fee for the engineers who designed the system would be an 'utter impossibility' for the tiny town. The people would still be faced with yearly payments exceeding $100,000. I don't have the slightest idea where such money is to come from. Even if we could get a federal grant to cover 75 percent, West Aaron obviously cannot afford the system." When contacted by the state capitol, a representative of the Commonwealth Environmental Agency stated that he had no knowledge of West Aaron's problem, but the new law applied to all towns with a population greater than 300.

Tonight's planning commission meeting was fairly routine. A little old lady wants to place her mobile home on a site that lacks a public water supply and is not connected to the regional sewage system. The lot has only 12,000 square feet, while 30,000 square feet are required in this zone. A farmer has illegally subdivided his farm by transferring two lots of an acre each to his sons and now wishes to accommodate his daughter and son-in-law with an acre lot. A six-pack store owner wishes to get final approval for the planting design around his recently enlarged establishment. A member of the regional planning staff wishes to discuss with us a 191 page report on economic growth. The supervisors wish us to study possible sites for a township garage. The citizen's association opposes an extension of Pleasant Valley Drive. Walter Hammond has written another fifteen-page letter explaining how the traffic-flow pattern in the region could better be improved on football weekends. A complaint from the Church of God. The entrance to their Sunday School building faces the screen of the Skylight Drive-in, which shows movies such as "The Nymphomaniac's Revenge" and "Gay-all-the-Way." We will invite Rev. Roger Gotwald to our next meeting to further discuss the problem.

The only hot spot is the session with Gilbert Walck, the district construction supervisor from J-Market. After about eight months of review and negotiation by the regional planning staff, our planning commission, and our supervisors, the plans for the first phase of the J-Market Shopping Center were approved with strict stipulations regarding the site design. Phase I includes a major department store and three specialty stores; Phase II will have a chain supermarket and other stores; Phase II presently is not defined. The approved plans call for parking clusters. By having the stores built at three levels, a minimum disturbance was to be inflicted on the site and also the drainage problems were to be minimized.

The questions I asked tonight were "why were all the trees cleared from the J-Market site?" "Why has some 50,000 tons of fill been removed from the site?" "Why was the drainageway filled?" And "why was construction started on Phase III which does not have final approval?" Walck replied, "I am not familiar with all the regulations of your township, but I have here a revised plan which will show you what we have done. We found that it was necessary to make certain field adjustments. Because we used a nonunion grading contractor, we decided to go ahead and have the grading done for Phases II and III before we moved the general construction workers on the site, since they are all union. We called the regional planning office and were told that we must go to the township supervisors to change the plan. So I called the chairman of the supervisors and he told me to call the township engineer; I could not get hold of him, so I asked our grading contractor to see to it. He told me it was OK. Of course I am sure he checked with your engineer. This job is only one of five $3,000,000 jobs that I'm working on and I cannot take care of all the details." I thought to myself, "No way are 50,000 tons of fill going to be returned nor will the trees be restored to the site. In the end those bastards from J-Market got their asphalt parking lot." Mr. Walck's final word for tonight was, "We have not hurt the ecology of the area! We are for ecology like everybody else."

CHAPTER 4

People Who Prey Together Stay Together

My alumni newsletter of last March reported the death of Orange Crate Otto. Orange Crate was better known by the students of my alma mater than any professors, campus leaders, or even the college president. For some forty years, Orange Crate operated a pushcart and sold oranges, apples, candy, and other items from his regular location near the library. He attended nearly every sporting event and was the college's most loyal fan. When a team had a losing season, Orange Crate conducted his version of a moral-boosting program for the teams and the rest of the student body with cheering sessions during the passage time between classes.

His real name was Otto Werner; he emigrated from Germany shortly after World War I. No one quite knew why he elected to live in a small college town. There were many mysteries about Otto. However, I did get to know him slightly better than most students. He lived in a garage that had been converted into a small cottage which he rented from my landlady. Otto knew all the athletes by name and many other students as well. He would sometimes drink a beer with the students, but never more than two; we thought he didn't want to set "a bad example for the freshmen." He treated everyone with respect; it was never Jim or Bob, but it was Mister Taylor or Mister Baker; the college teachers were Doctor Hall, Professor Spencer or Herr Professor Doktor Snyder for the German faculty. Otto had a way of being respectful that made you feel like you were a Rhodes Scholar.

On a number of occasions the students came to the defense of Otto. His title of "Orange Crate" arose from his habit during the winter months of burning wooden crates in a brazier made from an old metal barrel. On cold days the students would sometimes warm their fingers over his fire. The city council passed antipollution ordinances in 1970 and Otto was the first person arrested for pollution. He was arrested by a zealous policeman who disliked college people. The students protested that the local factories produced vast amounts of pollutants and were not checked; but Otto believed that law is law and must be obeyed. One very cold day in December, the students noticed that Otto was not at his usual post. An investigation by the student newspaper discovered that Otto was hospitalized with pneumonia. The paper led a campaign to raise funds with which thermal socks and underwear were purchased for Otto.

Since the obituary in the alumni newsletter was sketchy, I wrote to my former landlady for further details. I learned that five months previous to his death, Otto had been hit by a car while he was crossing at an intersection. My former landlady said that the papers reported "Otto was intoxicated and walked right into the path of a car driven by the son of Judge Cannon." She said it was common knowledge that it was the "Judge's son who was drunk and that the courts delayed all action relating to the accident until Otto died." Otto suffered two very shattered legs which were "botched-up by the local doctor"; again according to my former landlady, "between the neglect of the nursing home and the doctor, Otto died of a bone infection." She also said that "the nursing home and the doctor got $11,628.00 of Otto's savings and that $8,263.57, the residue of his estate, was willed to the college athletic fund."

I was angered by my former landlady's account of Otto's treatment, but not surprised. That community like so many small to medium-sized communities is ruled by a country-club Costra Nostra. The lawyers, judges, state attorney, many physicians and dentists, realtors, and other greedy businessmen have a closed fraternity. Usually they are members of the oldest local country club. After eighteen holes, they meet in the cocktail lounge to scheme against the Otto Werners.

Locally and currently the Verdant Hills Country Club has an appeal against Russell Township's decision to limit density in a proposed Verdant Hills planned residential development. The Verdant Hills Development Association maintains that it should be allowed 950 residential units, while the township has limited the development to a maximum of 520 units. The controversy centers around how the maximum density should be computed. Verdant Hills believes the density should be computed using their private golf-course lands as part of the open space, while the Russell planning commission contends that the golf-course land will not be available to the residents of the development unless they are also members of the private Verdant Hills Club, which is a commercial venture. In its suit, Verdant Hills maintains that the decision of the township planning commission and the supervisors was "arbitrary, capricious, abusive of discretion and contrary to law." Verdant Hills also claims that those who are most keenly interested in this plan are residents who presently do not live there because the development has not yet been built. Because of this, they cannot testify in defense of the Verdant Hills plan. What the country club wants to do is sell its surplus of land so that it can use the income from these sales to build an extravagant new clubhouse.

Interestingly, Judge Winston Raymond who will hear the case, the attorney for the country club, and the solicitor for the township are all members of the Verdant Hills Country Club. My father used to say, "law makes sense, but lawyers make cents."

Six months ago, our township lost a zoning case before the same judge; it was concerned with a request to extend a nonconforming blacktop-manufacturing operation into an area zoned R2 residential. The judge found in favor of the blacktopper. A week previous to the hearing, the judge and the owner of the blacktopper golfed together in the Virgin Islands; an ugly rumor claims that the judge's vacation was not paid for by the judge. A janitor friend who works at the courthouse observed that inmates at the county jail represent a better element than those who work in the courtrooms. Judges and lawyers forget that janitors have ears and eyes too.

Last year, I wrote a letter to the newspaper editor concerned with the morality of a local bookstore that sold books on how to manufacture LSD and grow marijuana while high schoolers were being jailed for only following instructions in the books. I asked a lawyer to read the letter first; he recommended that I not publish the letter. I later found that the lawyer also represented the bookstore and the newspaper. The editor of the newspaper and the state attorneys whom I requested look into the matter of the books on drug production are all Verdant Hills Club members. The reporters on the local papers all play games about protecting the public from elected officials, but never radiate a ray of sunshine on the businesses that advertise in the papers—a total eclipse.

Tonight I really wonder about lawyers. For six months we have looked at all means and schemes for preserving agricultural land in our township. We considered ten-acre minimum-size lots, developmental rights, and all the new ideas discussed at the recent planning conventions. Our final attempt is to allow all agricultural uses by right in an A1 (agricultural) zone and to restrict non-agricultural use to other than 1st class and 2nd class agricultural soils. We already base our flood-plain zoning on soil classification and a recent state referendum establishes "a clean and green" program for the state. In a six page letter, our solicitor advises us that "while preservation of usable agricultural land is apparently a valid goal for zoning, the various appellate courts have set few guidelines as to how this may be properly done. Zoning regulations are invalidated by the courts in cases where standards are not established by which administrative action can be properly measured. The standard should always be as definite as the circumstances will permit, otherwise denial by a conditional use could be deemed arbitrary and discriminatory, etc., etc., etc. After six pages, I am not sure what he has said; but I assume that it means he isn't sure and the law doesn't clearly establish a means of preserving agricultural land although the state constitution requires that it be done. Quite by chance the solicitor has just purchased a farm in our township.

My wife and I recently visited her Aunt Margie and Uncle Robert. They live in an older section of the City's Westside which is slated for redevelopment. Margie is fifty-nine years old and Robert is sixty-one. They operated a small restaurant until nine years ago, at which time they sold it and bought the apartment building in which they live; the building has three other apartments besides theirs. They provide for themselves by the income from the apartments, interest on their savings, and from a monthly Social Security check; Uncle Robert keeps busy doing minor repairs on the building. Their apartment building and the rest of their neighborhood will soon be taken over by the City Housing and Redevelopment Authority for construction of public housing. Margie and Robert paid $66,000 for the building nine years ago and still owe about $47,000. The Authority will pay Margie and Robert $98,250 for the building. However, they now must move to a new neighborhood; it is unlikely that they will be able to buy a similar building for less than $130,000. At their age, they will probably not be able to get another loan, and certainly not at 6 percent interest.

Of course, some of the people had tried to fight the redevelopment program, but the absentee landlords who saw a good chance to make some money did not support the community and the realtors started rumors about blacks moving into the neighborhood so the people who could do so got out. The blacks used to fear the KKK boogie of the Old South; now the Northerners cower behind locked doors, terrified of an imaginary black sheet. The blacks of the Old South and the present-day Northerners were and are being used by greedy people.

I just heard the claim that our planning commission turned a neat profit for the West Central Railroad without our knowing it. The railroad proposed abandoning its unused right-of-way six months ago; we have tried to arrange a meeting with the railroad to no avail. We were put off, had meetings cancelled, and were stalled for the whole period. The state public utilities commission approved of the abandonment just last week. The regional planning commission was considering using the right-of-way as a hike-bike trail. However, the West Central officials had talked to the landowners adjoining the right-of-way previous to the approval by the utilities commission and told the landowners that if they didn't agree to pay their rather high prices, that the planning commission was going to get the land and was going to establish a trail for motorcycles and snowmobiles to run on the old railroad bed.

The major problem of democracy is verbosity. There are always one or two members of any governmental body who find it necessary to more fully explain their position which is already fully understood by everyone else. God knows a person who concerns himself with public affairs must spend far too much time in meetings, but cannot he be spared excessive verbalizing? There certainly must be freedom from committee meetings in heaven.

Tonight was budget hearing night before the regional council of governments. I almost left before the hearing on the planning commission's budget because of the reception received by the library and police budgets. The library's major budgetary problem relates to federal revenue sharing. In the previous years, the library got $4,532 directly from special, earmarked library funds; this year those funds were made a part of the region's revenue sharing grant. The library requested $3,500 of revenue sharing funds from local government. Council member Clay Richardson, who is an administrator of a private research laboratory, Warren T. Maxwell, and David Beck, a technical representative for an equipment company, have been at the library staff and the chairman of the library board for nearly an hour. With questions, "How much does the average book cost?" "About $9.00." "Why do books cost so much? I can buy a paperback at the drugstore for $.75." I thought to myself, "You stupid bastards, have you read any books since you graduated from school?" "How many books do you have in the library?" "About 22,400 items." "Why do we need to buy 1,500 more books this year? Has anyone read all 22,400 books yet? How many people use the library anyway?" "About 38 per-cent of all citizens in this region." If I didn't have to defend the planning commission budget next, I would have swung at those Neanderthals. The same three yo-yos tried to sneak through the approval of an expansion of a local airport last September when they knew that most of those opposed to airport expansion were out of town on vacation between college terms. I find their parsimony and grandstand-ing over saving public tax dollars on the library budget hard to take when they wanted to use $90,000 of the revenue sharing funds for an airport that is used by only about 5 percent of the people in the region.

Even more distressing is the way Richardson, who is supposed to be trained in personnel administration, debases the public employees to the press. He cannot say, "We have a good police department which is giving us good service, but unfortunately we can only raise the budget for this department by 5 percent, because we just didn't have additional funds." NO! He must say, "We gotta stop these greedy cops from sopping up all the gravy." Even the most basic textbook on personnel administration suggests more tact. Of course, with Richardson's view of the library budget, it isn't very likely that he's looked at any modern text on personnel administration.

According to J. M. Barrie, "When Peter Pan helped-up Captain Hook and was bitten for his good manners, Peter was temporarily dazed and horrified. However, he, like no one else, quickly forgot each such experience. No one really gets over his first and each successive experience with unfairness, except Peter. This was the real cause of Peter's failure to grow up."

If, when I go to the supermarket, get my cart full of groceries including green peppers at two for 35¢, and then get yelled at for not having the peppers weighed (sometimes they sell peppers by the pepper and other times by the pound), I simply push my cart down some aisle and leave it and go to some other store. If I get

cheated out of change or an ice cream by a
vending machine, I simply pull the electrical
plug and get my revenge by envisioning the ex-
pression on the face of the vending man when
he sees the ice cream dripping out of his machine the next day. The supermarket is big and
unconcerned with me and the vending machine isn't concerned with the fact that it took
my last 15¢ and I didn't have lunch today.

In the big cities the schools are generally
controlled by a single board and a centralized
administration. Often this results in a failure to
appreciate priorities. I attended a lecture at
such a high school, the lecture was scheduled
from 7:30 to 9:30 P.M. and the topic proved to
be so stimulating that the audience wanted to
ask questions. At 9:35 P.M., a janitor walked in
and told everyone "Get the hell out in five minutes or I'll have the police throw you out." The
building maintenance union was so strong that
they believed the school was being run for their
convenience.

My first memorable encounter with injustice
occurred in first grade. The school bully beat
up the smallest kid; this I observed from a

distance. Of course, the kid cried and started to run to the teacher. The bully then stopped the kid and held an inquisition to determine who was guilty of beating the little kid. The bully lined up all the first to fourth graders, excluding himself and the little kid. All those in the line-up were required to place hands in front, palms down. The bully then hit each lined up kid, stating that if anyone hit him back it was evidence of guilt of hitting the littlest kid. When my turn came, I hit the bully in the nose. Thus proven guilty, I was held by the bully and the other students and beaten by the littlest kid.

It is reported that bomber pilots are generally not remorseful about dropping bombs on enemy cities, even though they may kill thousands of men, women, and children. The pilots are simply following their instructions and they are so far removed from the results of their action that the death and suffering they cause is not real. This is also true for a considerable portion of America's politicians, bureaucrats, big businessmen, and other large institutions. The procedures for handling different situations are neatly spelled out by regulations and protocol. Thus, people starve, lose jobs, suffer physical and mental pain, and are otherwise brutalized because of indifference, lack of responsibility, and organized greed. Don't look up; they have just pulled the rip-off cord and blivits are dropping.

CHAPTER 5

Prime Land Ripe for Development

A special hearing tonight on our proposed new zoning map. Nearly two hundred people, each with an axe to grind. Our old zoning map is hopelessly outdated and a mishmash of irreconcilable compromises. The first zoning regulations for the township were hastily drawn up by a consultant who didn't know the area, and were approved by a lay planning commission that didn't recognize the pitfalls of overzoning.

Tonight's proposed new zoning map is based on eight years of experience in fighting developers, many hundreds of hours of discussion and rewriting of the zoning ordinance, considerable advice from a professional planning staff, and the establishment of meaningful

85

long-range goals for our township and for the rest of the region. One major difference between our new zoning map and the old one is that we propose conservation zones for natural areas, farms, and flood plains; thereby we would drastically reduce potential development in rural areas.

This means that some five or six older farmers are angry, because they support their retirement by selling acre lots off the fronts of their farms. Two mobile home park developers are furious because they will not be able to use land on which they have options, since mobile home parks will not be allowed in the conservation zones. Developers, realtors, various businesses, and everybody else who exploits the area are up in arms. Tonight the only friend the planning commission has is the representative from the League of Women Voters.

When I joined the planning commission, the township had 10 ordinances and 3,542 people; today there are 106 ordinances and 8,905 residents. Somehow things worked out better with only 10 ordinances, except that sewage stood in the lawns in some subdivisions, 56 home owners got their water from cisterns, and there were no police and only limited fire protection. Most housing construction was substandard, developers only constructed gravel roads in their subdivisions, and the main township road was a honky-tonk of flashing neon signs. To a much lesser degree some of these problems persist, but most of the people in the township have the basic public services—sewers, water, parks, public buses, a five-man police department, better fire protection, paved streets, regular garbage collection, and other civilized public services.

The real fight tonight is not over strip commercial, planned residential, or flood plains, but over "what land is." To the farmer, land represents the source of his income. That land usually has been in his family for generations and he has plowed it, planted it, and lived on it all of his life. This land is his by right and sweat. The realtors, developers, and businessmen consider land a commercial product to buy and sell like hair tonic. For sale—105 acres of *prime* commercial land *ripe* for development—prime like a steak and ripe like a melon. The sensitive or the sentimental businessman may regret the destruction of a lovely old farmstead or a woodland where he hunted when he was a boy, *but progress cannot be stopped*.

Progress means an advance toward perfection. Toward what higher state is America moving? Cities immobilized by fear? A cloud of smog, smoke, and fumes? A listless, rootless society? A floundering bureaucracy? A conglomerate of greed?

I took my daughter to New York to see the Statue of Liberty, Central Park, and other sites. Central Park has probably been coveted by more schemers than any other piece of real estate in the United States. Since construction started in 1863, Frederick Olmsted, the park's designer, and later the several preservation associations that have concerned themselves with Central Park's integrity, have faced constant pressure "to improve the park." One early critic complained that the crooked roads in the park were unsafe for driving fast horses with light vehicles. There have been sincere and concerted efforts to convert Central Park into a lake for steamboat racing, a garage for 30,000 automobiles, an outdoor theater for 100,000, a tomb for General Grant, a model map of the

United States with miniature states, lakes, rivers, and mountains, a permanent circus grounds, an airport, an experimental farm, a speeding track for horses, a cemetery for distinguished Americans, and a site for each religious sect to construct a place of worship. If the recreation people had had their way, Central Park would be a jumble of Turkish baths, croquet grounds, rifle ranges, skating rinks, mineral springs, tennis courts, archery ranges, football fields, sandboxes, baseball fields, and kite-flying areas. Others would have covered Central Park with statues, water fountains, pavilions, pagodas, sidewalks, museums, restaurants, schools, hospitals, streets, railroads, and trolley tracks. As it is, Central Park has been intruded upon by an art museum, a restaurant, a skating rink, an open-air theater, a zoo, muggers, deviants, and dogs. There are many who would further exploit Central Park. "What is the use of a place filled with deviants and drug pushers? Sell it off and build highrises."

Anyone who has served on park boards, planning commissions, or similar agencies has fought and refought many battles with developers and other encroachers. They have many faces—at least two each. I have a friend who is a member of a militant conservation organization; he headed the fight against a power company that wanted to construct a power line across Mount Norman; however, my friend is a skier and recently supported the construction of a ski slope on the same *mountain*.

The garden club wants parks stocked with rose bushes while the police commissioner wants all the undergrowth removed so that nothing can go on in the bushes. One little old lady complains about pigeon's bombing statues and another wants to feed the pigeons.

Three volumes, 796 pages of words and maps to be discussed tonight. It has taken nearly five years for the parks and recreation staff and the regional planning staff to develop a park and open space plan for the region. The plan is excellent and generally well thought out, and if all goes well it will be approved and maybe even to a considerable degree be implemented, if state and federal funds can be obtained. Still, how do you face the greed of the pigmy baseball leaguers who believe that every boy must have tendonitis of the elbow? The park board members think I am crazy because I want the parks and open space to be zoned by use. I don't believe that recreation people can be trusted to protect natural areas. Most recreationists are consumers of land, with a fixation for grass and order. Tennis players look only for open courts and equestrians think only of trails and stables. First the recreational people remove dead logs to make woodland more attractive and then remove fallen leaves to make things neat, and then they selectively remove "undesirable trees," then they plant grass, then come picnic tables, and more trees are removed to make a baseball field for the picnic-table users.

An important leisure activity of the residents and visitors to a neighboring town is feeding the trout that are stocked in the water flowing from a large spring located near the downtown area. A few years ago the city fathers installed coin-operated fish-food dispensers near the spring; shortly two local merchants requested the removal of fish-food dispensers; they claimed that their sales of bread to the fish feeders greatly fell off and that the town fathers had no right to enter the fish-food business.

In natural environments the trail system and

the watering hole are major points of interaction between mammals. Many individuals and species use and "maintain a trail by use" and usually several trails lead to a watering hole; here is a kind of neutral ground with interaction and sharing. If we consider the pedestrian street to be a human trail, and fish ponds, duck ponds, flowing water fountains, sidewalk cafes, and other similar meeting places to be a kind of urban watering hole, we can draw a useful parallel. Unlike most great European cities, American cities lack "watering holes."

In our community duck watching is a chief recreational activity for many people. My wife and I took our four year old daughter to the pond to feed the ducks a couple of months ago. My daughter had some bread which she shared with the ducks, but also with some other children so that they could feed the ducks. Sharing and caring is an important experience for children. The children started talking to one another and playing together. My wife talked to another mother about children and then other things. The ducks served as a catalyst to bring strangers together—something greatly needed by urban Americans.

This duck pond is more intensely used than any park area in the region; however, it is not an official park; the ducks were promiscuously released and thereafter grossly neglected. The pond and surrounding land equals less than two acres, are poorly located from the viewpoint of accessibility, are not maintained in any sense, and are repeatedly threatened to be taken for a highway right-of-way or for some utilitarian use. The public somehow by protest and by luck has fought off the encroachers. Still the recreation-minded park board has not gotten the message that the people want a public watering hole.

In city parks in Amsterdam, I have observed flocks of sheep and herds of deer on islands. You can look across the landscape and see large animals peacefully grazing. However, many parks in small American towns are merely struggling grass beneath a stand of trees, a water fountain, and the remains of a bandstand, left from the days of outdoor concerts. These parks are used neither for children nor wildlife, except for starlings and a robin or two or an occasional bluejay. The alternative seems to be a park that is stuffed with sandboxes, swings, slides, and seesaws. Parks do not have to be dull to be safe nor are children the only people who need parks. Maybe not enough thought has gone into park design. Certain areas could be planted to prickles— hawthorn, cactus, and other "armed" plants and thus provide cover for birds. No sex maniac can commit rape on a bed of thorns. On the other hand, maybe there are weirdos who do this for their thing.

Yet another fight with the transportation department—this afternoon we walked the proposed realignment of a 0.6 mile section of Route 176. Eleven years ago, the department held a hearing with almost no fanfare. Since then the two farms most directly affected have changed ownership, three single-family homes have been constructed in the vicinity of the planned realignment, and two of the three township officials who reviewed the plans eleven years ago have moved out of the state. The 0.6 mile section has a sharp curve at a point where the road crosses a stream. About four times a year, a large truck fails to negotiate the curve properly and smashes the guard rails on the bridge. About two months later, the trans-

portation department repairs the bridge, restoring it to precisely the way it was before the
accident. A modest alternation of the bridge,
which wouldn't cost more than a few thousand
dollars, is all that is needed to effectively reduce
the accidents. However, the transportation department has an elegant $452,000 solution that
destroys the barnyard pasturage of two farms,
alters the course of a stream, replaces the old
metal bridge with a large concrete one, and
wastes the front lawns of three homes. No one
in the community really wants their solution
but since a hearing was held eleven years ago
there is no way of diverting the transportation
people from their grand purpose.

Tonight a developer brought in a plan for a
low-income housing project to be developed
out in the country. He argued that low-income
people have a right to a place to raise a family
and to have their own gardens. His solution to
low-income housing is to sell 80' × 100' lots
without a community sewer or water system
and with unpaved streets without curbs to keep
development costs down. He said, "We want to
have the kind of community where children
can grow up seeing nature." The first section of

the proposed development had one street named Nowata; the developer explained it was an American Indian name. A member of our planning commission whispered in my ear, "in section two, the streets will be named Nose-wera, Noparka, and Potholawantomie." The plan for this rural slum was drawn up by a moonlighting university landscape architect who just last week gave a lecture to a planning class; his subject was "The Responsibility of the Professional Planner to the Community."

In order for low-income housing to be acceptable to the general public in the U.S., the buildings must look poor and smell poor. Even a cheap grade of deodorant must be used in the insecticide for the control of cockroaches in this housing. The poor must be kept in their place and made to grovel. Deprived of their pride, weary with surviving, and subject to constant rip-offs, one cannot expect inmates of public housing to bestow beatitudes generously on public officials. When a window is broken or some equipment requires replacement, the length of time before repairs are carried out serves as a type of penitence for being poor, and also proves to the general public that people on welfare destroy property. Architects must have special training to know that 8' × 9' bedrooms and fewer closets better meet the needs of people with low incomes. Middle-class Americans want the welfare recipient to wear a scarlet "P" on his chest.

I once heard a bright young architect lecture that it is possible to design housing that will cause crime, divorce, and family strife. Little does he know that many housing authorities and private companies are already in this business. In their rush for cheap and quick solutions, the urban political leaders have sanctioned the construction of housing that does not meet human needs; so that the general public is not contaminated, public housing must be isolated from the middle class to maintain their purity. Things are much worse in a university community, where even the bluecollar workers are considered to be lepers and must wear an "I" for ignorant. It should be a requirement that those who teach sanitary engineering spend one day a month emptying cesspools, those who teach agriculture spend their day cleaning a pig yard, those who teach psychology spend their day in an insane asylum, and those who teach law be locked in the county jail.

In a very transient community, in ten years I have seen one complete turnover in planning staff and two and a half changes in planning commission members, and three complete changes of supervisors; one saving factor was that three planning commission members were elevated to be supervisors to fill unexpired terms. The remarkable thing is that a "gung-ho" chamber of commerce type, when appointed to the planning commission, transmutes into an enlightened planner so quickly; the reformers, when elected to office, antagonize the liberals who elected them by becoming more conservative and aware of how things really function.

Seemingly simple problems become complex and take months and even years to solve. More than half of the problems that we discussed during my first year on the planning commission are still on this year's agenda.

A friend of mine who belonged to the same bridge club for twenty-five years, claimed that the people who won the table prizes twenty-five years ago are still winning the prizes today, and the losers are still trumping their partner's aces. People all talk a great deal about self-improvement, but do very little about it. Developers promise a lot, but deliver far less. Planning commissions also do a lot of talking. If they are a good commission, they also do a good deal of listening. When the vibrations are right, things can happen. It takes a lot of persuasion and sometimes a good clump to get plans to become realities; sometimes nothing works.

A luncheon meeting today; this time to discuss problems associated with Smitty's salvage yard. He is a primitive who poked the county sheriff in the nose for trying to repossess an electric stove. Our ordinances require screening around junkyards; the area has been zoned R3 high density residential since 1963, when our zoning ordinance was adopted. Since the salvage operation came into existence in 1966, Smith is clearly in violation of the ordinance. However, Mr. Smith regularly gives marvelous pleas for free enterprise, screams, cries, and regularly cusses out every township official and judge; he is a throwback to Huckleberry Finn's father. This time he drove the code inspector off his property with a pistol; he accused the inspector of stealing hub caps. His neighbor, Dusty Pepper, across the highway, operates a carelessly constructed shopping center and drive-in theater which partially burned down last month; it was started in 1961 on an "open-ended" building permit. The tract of land houses a vacated gas station, a hoagy shop, a trailer park, a drive-in theater, and scattered stores which seem to burn down regularly. There have been at least six unexplained fires that I remember. Some neighbors claim that the fires are caused by spontaneous generation from the sex movies shown at the drive-in.

The quickest way to orient strangers to our township is to mention Smitty's salvage yard and Dusty's shopping center. We never seem to enforce any township ordinances against that pair. We thought we had Smitty once, but our solicitor blew it by accepting a compromise; when you compromise with Smitty you suffer a gradual defeat rather than a total rout. The results of our discussion is that our solicitor will inform Smitty by registered letter that he must comply with the screening ordinance. I am sure that postman who delivers this letter will earn a citation of valor for this noble act.

As I drive past Dusty's shopping center on my way back to work, I note that he is moving materials around; I am sure that he would not start reconstruction without a new building permit. But perhaps I had better keep my lunch times free for next week.

A letter in this morning's paper from a Stanley Jones claims our planning commission "is harassing Mr. Willard Smith" and that he is our "whipping boy." We are accused of "hiding behind a blizzard of obscure legalisms." We are told that, "reputable businessmen should be left in peace so that they may provide the required services to our healthy, growing community." Would the real Mr. Jones please stand up?

Many failures of planning occur in the execution—partly by dupery, partly by incompetency, and partly because of negligence. Duplex houses are built in the flood plain in a single-family zone. But after such $65,000 monsters are a reality what can one do? Have them torn down or hope that when the deluge comes, the dwellers in this duplex have been thoughtful enough to have on board a representative pair of each species of their families? The fault for such diluvial disasters can often be laid upon the builder who had the building half constructed before he applied for a building permit, or upon a township engineer who was busy and issued a permit without looking at the site. The planning commission is stuck and the renters of the duplex at least have the novelty of frogs in their playrooms.

Regulations can only prescribe minimums. Houses today are built with $2'' \times 4''$ frames and not oak beams. Is a house a family resource that is passed from one generation to the next? Or is it a consumable? Repairs, improvement, and alterations to adapt the structure to unique family situations are not made; the family must fit the house, not the house the family. This is one reason why people move and communities are unstable; houses are not built to change. Construction costs are more important than maintenance costs. A house that will last 200 years and one that will last 15 years may differ only 10 to 20 percent in construction materials. However, banks and tax laws treat the two cases the same. The person who builds a structure that will last 200 years should have a lower rate of taxation and better loan arrangements from the banks than someone who builds a self-destructing dwelling. The basic resources (such as lumber and steel) are being grossly wasted in the self-destructing house.

Similarly, the farmer who improves the soil and his buildings, thus maintaining and creating a resource, is more heavily taxed than someone who is mismanaging the soil and destroying future resources. Our tax system, and to a large degree our economic system, rewards the greedy and forces the frugal to dishonesty and a compromise of their ideals.

A problem of political office is that of separation of public life from private life. A serious symptom, not to be lightly ignored, occurs when a politician believes that he must retain his office, or seek a higher office, because he is so much better than the other likely candidate. Even more fatal is the belief that only he can carry out the will of the people; this is only one step away from, "what is good for me is good for my community."

I once worked for a man who owned a company that sold office supplies. He required his salesmen to change their white shirts twice daily; the office force were to have only one paper on their desk tops at a time and to have their telephones in the exact same location on each desk. Everyone sat tall, so they could think tall. He was rich and gave his formula full credit for his success. He also owned a swine farm and applied the same formula to the pigs, who were not as cooperative as his salesmen about neatness and sitting tall. He, like many administrators, held to a single rigid formula and attempted to fit everyone and everything into it. This is too often the problem with bureaucrats; the reports and forms are more important than the results; appearance is all.

At our most recent election, one candidate's only platform pledge was "I'm going down to the state capitol and knock those bureaucratic heads together and get some action for my district." Little does he know how isolated most institutions are against achievement and change. When he gets to the capitol he will be rudely shocked.

Land-use planning is resented by those with political power. Most of the land-use programs in the United States have been paper tigers. The United States Department of Agriculture has many programs yielding inventory data on natural resources—soil, water, and on the plants and animals. The USDA also promises technical assistance to farmers and planning groups in carrying out some hundreds of kinds of land-use projects. Their promises look great in handouts and in annual reports, but in the end, you get a fizzle. Federal agencies don't have the manpower or understanding of local conditions to get results. State agencies also come on strong, but quickly fade. We have tried to close a mobile home park in our township for five years on reports from the state sanitarian; whenever we are ready to go to court, the sanitarian backs off. Still the neighborhood dogs dine on the sewage which overflows from the mobile homes.

The dilemma of protecting people from the unscrupulous and from their own ignorance is not easily solved. I know of a community of about 100 houses of which more than 50 percent will become infested with termites within ten years. It will cost about half of the 100 home owners a total of approximately $25,000 to have their homes treated for termites, plus the cost of repairing damage. If the houses had all been pretreated for termites during construction, the total cost would have been $7,500. Pretreatment for termites could have been written into the building-code ordinances; in fact, pretreatment requirements could have been inserted into our township and no one would have raised an objection, because so few of us were involved in the adoption and revision of the codes. But, how far do you go in providing protection? The reason houses have termites is, to a large degree, because of faulty construction. Afterwards sometimes unscrupulous fly-by-night pest-control companies treat little old ladies' homes for termites and charge extravagant prices. Do you enforce pretreatment for termites or do you educate the public? This dilemma of protection applies to many areas of human endeavor. How aware should the buyer be? If we allow land to be exploited, why not people?

Regulations have taken much of the joy out of life. When I was a kid, with my friends, cousins, brothers, I often went swimming three or more times a day. Sometimes we would swim two or three miles across the lake; other times we would roughhouse playing "king of the raft." There was no lack of things to do or explore in the water. This past summer I did not go swimming even once. I find no pleasure in the roped-off beaches or the oversized bathtubs in which one now must swim in order to be protected from drowning. None of my childhood friends drowned, because we respected the water and knew our abilities; those who drowned were city kids or drunks who neither respected the water nor knew their limitations. Must all physical activity be competitive and regulated by whistle-mouthed jocks? Disorganized, pick-up baseball games, neighborhood kickball, and polo played on work horses bring back pleasant memories. I don't believe that today's kids will look back with much recalled joy on the organized games they must play. There were certainly unhappy experiences in the time of my youth. We had our lows. But our highs were high and I don't recall that we were as chronically bored as is the claim of modern youth.

Yesterday a local merchant chopped down a maple in front of his store so that he could widen his driveway; the shade tree commission had previously refused him a permit to remove the tree. Today he thumbed his nose and told the shade tree commission to "stick it." My first reaction was, "I hope they really slap it to the bastard." However, I am not so sure about my first gut response. Why must every street be lined with the same-sized trees, each spaced forty feet apart? Since he was willing to plant a smaller tree fifteen feet away from his expanded driveway, why the big deal? George Washington murdered a tree and wasn't punished.

So many planning decisions are emotional ones. I have a hang-up on mobile homes. Only recently have I stopped calling them trailers. I lived in a trailer park many years ago and rescued one child from a trailer fire and saw another trailer burn up with children inside. To be sure, conventional homes burn. Are my votes on mobile home matters entirely rational? Probably not. Should they be? Most of the public responses to planning are emotional rather than rational. If a piece of land has not been developed, no one concerns themselves. However, when the trees are removed and the construction of a gas station commences on this piece of land, all the neighbors object, even if the style of the service station was designed to match the neighborhood. A new gas station should always be in the next block, a new highway in the next township, and new landfill in the next county.

The major problem with the general public is that until they see it happening they are not concerned. What planners fail to do is visualize different future alternatives for the public. A colored map denoting C-1 doesn't mean much to most people. However, if you selected the worst possible enterprises—like a stockyard or a buffalo chip embalmer—and indicated that such enterprises could be placed next to their $60,000 home, then maybe someone would understand.

I don't accept the argument that a public official, be he or she an elected official, an appointed lay adviser, or a paid public employee or administrator, has only to vote or push his bias. First the administrator must educate the lay advisers and the elected officials to new ideas and programs; then all of these must attempt to educate the public. There will then be reactions and ferment and often times a better answer than what would have occurred without public input. Educating the public is where we fall down. It is easier to pass laws than it is to inform and convince the general public what is best for them collectively or individually. We would need far fewer laws and we would have far more freedom, if we could do a better job of educating. Regulations make everyone the same; education makes everyone different. This is a lesson our Environmental Protection Agency might heed.

EPA is the worst offender at splitting hairs. A pest-control operator friend was recently cited for killing spiders in a warehouse; the pesticide he used according to the EPA inspector was approved for spider control in homes and a warehouse is not a home. A farmer was told he must construct a fence to enclose a creek in the middle of a cow pasture so that his cows would not pollute the stream. He told the federal agent "when you keep the deer and the fish from fouling up the stream, I'll fence my cows out."

Even with the expansion of EPA, there must not be enough nuts in Washington, D.C., because periodically a new batch of White House squirrels must be shipped to Virginia. The surplus squirrels cannot be destroyed because of possible unfavorable publicity, so they are sent south to eat nuts belonging to Virginia squirrels. No one has considered that the White House squirrels will most likely die because only so many squirrels can exist in a certain area. This solution seems to be a typical Washington solution; make a good show, never come to grips with the real problem, and shift the responsibility to the states and locals.

CHAPTER 6

A Lullaby of Turfland

In third grade, our class read *Evangeline*. One portion I recall vividly. "So passed the morning away. And lo! with a summons sonorous sounded the bell from its tower, and over the meadows a drum beat. Thronged ere long was the church with men. Without, in the church-yard, waited the women. They stood by the graves, and hung on the headstones garlands of autumn leaves and evergreens fresh from the forest." Our class, strongly influenced by impressions gained from Halloween and our preoccupation with telling ghost stories, thought that the poor Acadian women who had to wait for their men in the church cemetery must have been scared by the graves and ghosts. Our wise teacher said that an old church cemetery could be a beautiful place. She said that when she was young, children

113

played hide-and-seek behind the tombstones, young lovers walked hand in hand after church and showed each other where their ancestors were buried, and old people came on warm spring days to pay homage to departed friends. I can remember then how sad I thought the Acadian exiles must have been when they were forced to leave part of their family behind.

When I became interested in prairie plants, I found that many of the old country cemeteries sheltered asters, goldenrod, blazing star, blue-stem, compass plants, and other prairie remnants. When my mother and I became interested in family genealogy and local history, we found much pleasure in visiting church cemeteries. To find the essential data on the ancestor in question was only part of the satisfaction. We read inscriptions, noted important local family names, and found much on which to speculate tragedies, protests, and humor. At other times when I have wandered across family cemeteries, usually in a vintage stage of neglect, I have tried to imagine a story to go with the graveyard. My interest in the American Civil War has lead me to visit many battlefields and cemeteries. While I do not fancy myself a ghoul, I have taken a special interest in cemeteries.

Thus I had special interest in tonight's planning meeting. The Sunrise Memorial Park Association has requested a building permit for the construction of a spacious Garden Chapel Mausoleum. Thompson Summers, the chairman of the Memorial Park Association, showed us the plans for a marble structure with a red tile roof, designed in Spanish style. He told us how the first mausoleum was built in 353 B.C. for King Mausolus from whom we get the word mausoleum. We learned that mausoleums provide complete comfort and security for our loved one. This model will be constructed of granite, imported marble, California tile, bronze, steel, and reinforced concrete and will endure through the ages. The building will be heated and air-conditioned for the year-round comfort of the guests. The above-ground crypts are clean, dry, and well ventilated. Because of my interest, I asked about insects and was informed that there would be monthly, contracted pest-control services. Also, music would be piped into the chapel and one could request special songs to be played on Mother's

Day or on a birthday or have flowers delivered; these could be paid for with a charge account and the family would be billed directly. When Mr. Summers informed us that their only concern was to help families complete now the sacred duty that must sooner or later be fulfilled, we could not refuse him his building permit. After all, how much better to meet this inevitable obligation while members of the family are privileged to consult together. We certainly do not want anyone to suffer a lonely hour of confusion and not have "their house in order." That is just poor planning.

One thing that strikes me is that as we have become more and more urbanized, we have become divorced from our forefathers. The family and churchyard cemeteries have given way to community cemeteries planted with pines and located on hills just outside of town. The community cemeteries are larger, generally operated without a profit, and scarcely visited. In the minds of children, they are haunted. Gradually, commercially operated cemeteries have superseded the community and family types.

At first these commercial cemeteries were

monument cities with large, extravagant memorabilia. In the 1930s, landscape architects and cemetery designers, such as Howard E. Weed, came to the rescue. In a book on cemetery design, Weed observed that sod-covered graves, marked only by a simple stone sunk even with the turf, were best, because this is simplicity and in simplicity lies beauty and economy. He considered land of gently rolling character with sandy loam soils best for cemeteries, because grave-digging is easier and cheaper. Hilly sites are bad because of the added expense in grading drives and the increased costs of repairs. Stony stratum is absolutely unfit, because of difficulty in digging. To Weed, nothing was more restful and inviting to the eye than green grass, which is the most important ingredient for best lawn effects. Willow and weeping mulberry should be avoided, because they suggest sorrow without enhancing the landscape. Trees such as catalpa, cottonwood, and poplar are bad because they produce leaves and other litter which is costly to clean up. According to Weed, cemetery rules and regulations should prohibit anything that would be detrimental to appearance or would add to the costs of care. Also, all charges for interments, removals, foundations, or other work should be paid in advance. Based on this sound philosophy, modern cemeteries have replaced headstones with bronze markers; maintenance costs thereby have been greatly reduced; mowers can operate right over the markers. Also, modern cemeteries regulate the days when people can honor the dead; thereby trash-removal costs are decreased and further savings are realized. Ornamental plantings are kept to a minimum and closely pruned to reduce interference with mowing operations. Because there are so few song birds present, a carillon provides music when people are present. No longer cluttered by memorial stones, the modern cemetery is billed as unspoiled open space.

Today, cities are facing a serious shortage of burial sites. Calvary Cemetery in New York City has two million bodies crammed in 500 acres. An average cemetery can hold between 1,500 and 3,000 graves per acre. Because of lack of space, in some parts of the world, there are waiting lists for burial sites.

Certainly more efficient land use can be

made in most cemeteries. Double- and triple-layer interments, reselling unused plots, reuse of graves, vertical burial, cremation, and cemescrapers are all methods of accommodating more dead on less acreage. Many cities are building columbaria, cemetowers, cemescrapers, and concrete cities for the dead. Also old cemeteries in the center of cities are being exhumed and moved to the edge of the cities.

Those who have been concerned with the grave squeeze and the relocation of city cemeteries beyond the city limit have not really faced the problem of memorializing the dead. To my mind, when a person dies, he or she deserves better than to be dumped into a hole and run over regularly with a seven-gang mower with hydraulic controls. Moreover, there are some better solutions to the burial-memorializing problem than those currently in practice. First we must recognize that we cannot forestall our own death by moving the cemetery out of sight to some sunset park or rose-lawn rest. The continuance of the family, as evidenced by family and churchyard cemeteries, is broken by the memorial park; in such a place we do not think of our ancestors, except with passing guilt on Easter, Mother's Day, or Memorial Day. I have heard many voices say that the funeral industry is giving the public what it wants. This I don't believe. The pomp and expense of dying is increasing more rapidly than the cost of living, because there is no means by which the general public can avoid exploitation by the funeral industry. By and large, what the public wants is an inexpensive way of disposing of the body and an effective means of memorializing and preserving the memory of their relatives or friends. What they get is the opposite.

The recent presidents of the United States, Franklin Delano Roosevelt, Harry S Truman, Dwight David Eisenhower, John Fitzgerald Kennedy, and Lyndon Baines Johnson have all memorialized themselves with libraries that contain their papers and other memorabilia. In a democracy such as ours, even the most humble deserve more than a name and two dates chiseled on marble or granite or raised letters and numbers on a bronze marker.

When I was in London for about two weeks attending a conference, I used to cut through an old churchyard several times daily. Obviously this churchyard was a cemetery in which the gravestones had, with one exception, long since disappeared. Currently, the churchyard was being used by the local residents as a park. Young boys were practicing soccer, mothers were exercising their small ones, and older people were feeding the birds. Everytime I went through the park I thought, "this is the way all cemeteries should be." Instead of sticking the dead in barren plots away from life, create real memorial parks. Instead of stones and markers destroying the utility of the landscape, simply bury the people underneath and use the area above. If people need to have markers, a beautiful wall can be constructed around the park of blocks of granite. Inscriptions could be recorded on the granite blocks and records kept by a local historical society, church historical society, or a library building located in the park. Such records might only be the minimal accounting of the person's life or it might be an accumulation of poems, publications or newspaper clippings, or other contributions made by a person. The memorial facility or service would maintain the records of its community in the same manner as the prestigious libraries of the United States presidents, but for the average person.

Turf is a crop unlike agricultural crops. In growing turf, the baby is thrown away and the bathwater is kept. The clippings are harvested and discarded, and only the stubble is what is desired. In addition to the cemeteries, there are roughly 30 million home lawns, 65,000 elementary, secondary, college, and university campuses, 9,000 golf courses, 317 million miles of street and highway rights-of-way, plus grounds about industrial plants, public and private athletic fields, large portions of urban parks, and other, more minor turflands. Probably there are about 20 million acres of urban-type turf in the U.S. Much of this open space is little more than a lush, green, biological desert, populated by about 25 million Wheel Horses, Toros, International Cubs, Gravelys, and other mechanical herbivores. Considering that approximately 20,000 U.S. citizens suffer amputations, fractures, lacerations, and other gruesome injuries from these mechanical browsers each year, it might be safer to go back to "a home where the buffalo roam."

It has been estimated by several authorities

on bird life that there is an average of about one to two birds per acre in the United States. Audubon breeding bird censuses indicate that woodlands with diverse and adequate undergrowth will have four or five nesting birds per acre, while woodlands stripped of undergrowth will average a bird per acre or less. Most suburban and urban areas, as well as crop lands, average less than one bird per acre. Certain special habitats such as marshes, sloughs, bogs, and small ponds often support six or more nesting birds per acre; however, man has fetish for filling these with garbage and other debris.

Besides the resident bird population, any area will have various types of nonresidents. These may be migrants passing north or south, accidentals or strays that breed in nearby areas, winter visitors, or individuals that are attracted to an area by food, water, or other requirements. For example, a bird feeder may attract large numbers of birds at certain times, but they will not all be nesters.

When I moved to my present home, the only vegetation that was present was about a dozen trees and three and a half acres of poorly maintained turf. The former owner loved dogs, cats,

and mowers. For the first two years of my resi-
dency, I did not have the time to greatly alter
that landscape design. During these years there
were eight nesting birds—one year, a pair of
house wrens and a pair of robins; the next, a
pair of Baltimore orioles and again a pair of
house wrens. Also during this time, I saw no
more than twenty species of birds per year on
my property.

Presently, my land use is a half acre of orchard, a half acre of vineyard, a quarter acre of
garden, a quarter acre of brambles and other
small fruit, a half acre of weedy vegetation,
three quarters of an acre of sheep pasture, a
quarter acre of lawn, and half an acre of woodland. I do not have cats or dogs, but my neighbors keep these pets which visit us; also my
older daughter has a small flock of sheep.

By late fall my garden and edge areas are
fairly weedy; these weeds and the gardening
debris are left undisturbed during the winter. I
leave the dead trees and other tree remains
where they are in the developing woodland
area. I try not to be too greedy and allow
surpluses to remain on fruit plantings, use pes-
ticides with judgment, and tolerate some plant

injury in my orchard and garden from mice, rabbits, and other "pests." Last year, at least eighteen birds nested and I observed seventy species of birds on my property.

In addition, grey squirrels, red squirrels, chipmunks, deer mice, meadow mice, house mice, and short-tailed shrews are resident mammals. Cottontails, flying squirrels, jumping mice, red foxes, striped skunks, opossums, Norway rats, whitetail deer, and several species of bats are visitors. Recently, I have also seen a few snakes, salamanders, and frogs, and many toads. My property adjoins state gamelands, but only with habitat improvement did the numbers and kinds of wildlife increase on my three and a half acres. Some day I shall organize an urban land pool, in which thousands of people will join together to cooperatively manage their backyards in a massive birdification effort. Each property owner will be required to have at least 10 percent of his property in weeds.

It is apparent to me that the most important things that I did to improve the habitat for wildlife was to diversify the cover and to produce a crop of weed seeds and insects where only turf had been before. By the standards of my mother, I was a sloppy farmer, because I did not cut down the thistles, burdocks, pigweed, and other noxious plants.

My little plot demonstrates to me that the organization of most natural communities is exceedingly complex. The simplism that there is a balance of nature fails to convey the actual complexity of natural systems. Just a simple accounting of the number of species of plants and animals in a specific natural community is not enough to describe the immensity of alternatives within the community. A natural system is not static, but rather dynamic. An equilibrium resulting from two counteracting balancing forces is a naive conception. Whatever balance there is in a natural community is the result of many interacting forces.

The imagery of a web of life in a natural system gives more perspective. At the foundation level, green plants convert carbon dioxide and water, by means of the energy from the sun, into food stuffs that support the rest of the community. All other life is divided into various classes of consumers, among which are herbivores, omnivores, carnivores, and putrivores. Typical herbivores, such as cattle, deer, and grasshoppers, are general feeders; however, some plant feeders specialize and may consume only seeds, sap, roots, pollen, or other parts of plants. The omnivore is a generalized feeder, consuming many plant and animal materials; man is an example. Carnivores are meat feeders; and vary in size from lions to parasitic mites. Putrivores clean up wastes, recycle dead organisms, and return resources to the ecosystem.

A web of life suggests alternative consumption routes. For example, a particular deer mouse could be consumed by a hawk, a shrew, an owl, a cow, fly maggots, or any other of a number of consumers. However, this concept fails to account for the level of consumption. The imagery of biotic pyramid suggests that there are many small vegetarians at the bottom and a few large carnivores at the top. It takes about 300 mice per year to maintain one sparrow hawk. It is not a simple matter that a sparrow hawk requires so many prey for its support. If mice are scarce, small birds may represent alternate food. More importantly, the prey population must maintain a breeding population plus a harvestable surplus which is regularly consumed by the hawk. The ability of the mouse population to maintain such a hawk population is not only a function of its own reductivity, but of other organisms as well. An ecosystem is not neat and simple. The introduction of an exotic species, the mutation of a single gene, or the activities of man can greatly disrupt a natural community.

The activities of man are apparent when he urbanizes a forest, for example. One way of viewing a forest is as a series of layers. The topmost tier of a forest in the eastern United States is commonly called the upper canopy. Here the crowns of the tall trees interlock and interrupt penetration of light, at least during the foliage season. Beneath are tiers of lesser trees, low-level shrubby growth, and a ground cover of herby growth. The soil is covered by a layer of litter and duff with a zonation of life extending into the soil.

Man selects a site for his home in the forest because he wishes for the tranquil beauties of nature, bird songs, wild flowers. But what does he do to the natural community that supports these organisms? He removes and burns the leaves which are the means whereby nutriment is recycled and returned to the trees.

Garreth Eckbo, a landscape architect, observed, "In grasslands and prairies, we plant trees; in forests we clear open spaces and plant grass; in the desert we introduce both trees and grass. All of these changes have the function of equalizing, improving, and humanizing the landscapes, making them better places for us to live." Mankind is constantly affecting nature and seldom clearly recognizes that he is effecting changes. Raking the leaves each fall has a profound impact on a woodland, but nonetheless raking goes on without many people considering what may be the results.

The newly appointed shade tree commission met for the first time last night. They are now responsible for planting and maintaining the trees along the urban streets in the township. Wouldn't you know, Locust Lane will be planted to honey locust, Pine Street to white pines, and Birch Street to white birch. The members of the commission are a lady gardener, a landscaper, and an assistant professor of horticulture at the University. I would have thought that at least one of them would have learned the elm-tree lesson.

The American elm was planted as a street-and-lawn tree in much of the United States; often more than 90 percent of the trees in many midwestern cities were of this species. In the midwestern city where I spent many of my college years, the original population of American elms was 14,103 trees. Starting in 1944, a virus disease, phloem necrosis, infected elm trees; this disease is transmitted from tree to tree by leafhoppers. During the first five years of its presence, only a few trees were killed and the disease spread slowly. In 1951, Dutch elm disease, a fungus disease spread by a bark beetle, appeared on the scene. Between 1952 and 1961 nearly all the American elms were killed. The last time I was back to visit in 1969, only 56 of the original 14,103 trees remained; 78.7 percent, or 11,057, were killed by Dutch elm disease and 21.3 percent, or 2,990, were killed by phloem necrosis. The lesson of diversity seems to be a hard one to learn.

To a biologist concerned with the management and protection of the urban environment, almost every action of man has an impact on this system. There are many alternatives and it is necessary to develop a grand strategy. In the urban community, there is a dearth of trained environmentalists. Scientists who specialize in environmental biology usually have rural backgrounds and tend to associate with institutions away from urban surroundings. Urbanites who specialize in biology tend to go into such fields as physiology, public health, medicine, and biochemistry. Wildlife management has afforded major employment opportunities for environmental biologists. To a marked degree, studies of urban-wildlife and pest-management problems have been neglected. Unfortunately, most biologists who have experience in animal management attempt to fulfill their own needs for therapeutic outdoor activity and tend to work on cave salamanders in the Ozarks rather than cat fleas in New York City. As the general public has become aware in recent years, ecology is the branch of biological study that deals with the relationships between living organisms and their environment. The name of this scientific discipline is derived from two Greek words, *oikos* = household and *ology* = study. While the derivation of the word suggests a concern for domestic biological problems, most professional ecologists have directed their attention toward an understanding of animals and plants in natural settings, rather than about the home of man.

An ecologist is fundamentally an observer of natural systems. Unfortunately there are all too few observers of nature on the urban scene. This is not for want of observable material. The architect who expects trees to take root in a solidified aggregate of sand, gravel, and cement is not a good observer. The public-health officer who expects to control a major rat problem by use of rodenticides alone has not observed rodent populations. The bird lover who expects to have a downy woodpecker in his backyard cannot be too fastidious about how he goes about pruning his trees.

Many municipalities have very strict laws making it a serious offense to grow any plants but turf and trees. The ordinance for University City reads in part "No person, firm, partnership, or corporation owning or having a present interest in or occupying any real estate within the Borough limits shall permit any grass or weeds or vegetation whatever, not edible or planted for some useful or ornamental purpose to grow or remain on such premises, including any portion of the premises occupied by a street or alley, so as to exceed the height of six inches or to throw off any unpleasant or noxious odor or to conceal any filthy deposit or to create or produce pollen. All such vegetation is hereby declared to be a nuisance and detrimental to the health, safety, cleanliness, and comfort of the inhabitants of the Borough. . . ." On the surface, a weed-control law seems to serve a desirable purpose, but if enforced, prevents the production of a seed crop for birds and drastically reduces the available insect food needed by birds. Man with bulldozers, chain saws, lawnmowers, and other instruments of improvement can completely shatter a natural community. Most suburban and urban situations are fragments, bits and pieces, one or two tiers, skeletons, or refuse of previous ecosystems. We fail to see what a profound action we take when we mow our lawn twice weekly and keep our grounds as tidy as a grave. We seem to fear diversity.

CHAPTER 7

It's Raining Cats and Dogs

Man's experience with animals has been a long and rich one. Early man hunted animals with crude implements of wood and stone while other animals hunted man with teeth and claws. The domestication of plants encouraged a sedentary type of community life for man; pest species congregated to these communities, attacking man and his food reserves. The domestication of horses, camels, donkeys, and to a lesser degree cattle, goats, reindeer, buffalo, llamas, elephants, and dogs allowed man to transport foodstuffs, building materials, and to conduct wars and commerce. Without animals for transport and food, cities as we know them could not have come into being.

To a great degree, food has lost its identity. Premixed and prepackaged products bear little resemblance to their plant and animal origins.

Grains have become strangely shaped flakes, chips, and loops. Fruits and vegetables miraculously appear on store shelves without blemishes from pests or diseases, and without relationship to season. Rhubarb is no longer the first fruit of spring. The carnal aspects of our diet are concealed. The gory realities of slaughterhouses, butchers, and carcasses have been extricated from the flesh to become a protein-rich source, called chops, steaks, roasts, and burgers.

With the machine age, cars, trucks, buses, trains, and airplanes have almost completely replaced animals for urban transport; even more powerful instruments have replaced animals in warfare. Man the farmer has discarded crude animal-powered implements for specialized machines and advanced technology. Yet, the farmer on his tractor is a poorer observer of nature than his father with a team of horses. Plants, animals, and their products are produced with factorylike efficiency. Both rural and urban man have disassociated themselves from previously important aspects of their lives.

However, in each of us there is still a hunter

and a farmer. The sight of a doe nuzzling her fawn softens even the most callous of hearts. A flat of pansies for sale at the fruit store down the block elicits a desire within each of us to own a little piece of earth. A bit of our phylogenic history lingers in hidden niches of our minds.

This I see all about me in the city. As I drive to work, I find the streets crowded by Beetles, Cougars, Falcons, Stingrays, Barracudas, and Mustangs. My sports page informs me of the plight of Cubs, Bruins, Bears, Longhorns, Cardinals, Orioles, Dolphins, and that Jack Nicklaus hit an Eagle on the eighth green. In church, people worship a deity who is likened to a shepherd who leads his flock to green pastures, and whose son was born in a barn, attended by livestock. My friends inform me that they are "contented as a cow" or "happy as a lark" or "have girlfriends that mate like minks." On TV, bear, deer, lambs, and other animal life huckster for the nonpolluting oil companies. Lassie is eternal and pushes soup—or something else this year. As I walk down Main Street, the store windows are filled with multicolored rabbits, frogs, pandas, and alligators—bed companions for children and teenage girls. As I ponder a selection of Old Crow, Three Feathers, and White Horse at the corner liquor store, a Pig in the street with a Camel in his mouth directs traffic.

Ronnie Lovitt has opened a summer camp for dogs—no cats allowed. Camp Canino is located about 120 miles from the big city. The counselors at the camp are college majors in animal science with a love for dogs. Activities for the dogs include swimming, rough and quiet play, and squirrel chasing. The basic cost of camp is $175.00 per month which includes pickup for camp and home delivery after camp. For $100.00 extra per week, the dog can be trained in basic obedience and for $150.00 per week the dog can be trained in protection.

It is recommended that the dog be sent old shirts and socks from home periodically so it will not forget the smell of its master. Also, special doggy items, such as favorite toys, water dishes, and special foods, should be provided so the dog doesn't get homesick. Money should be sent from time to time for camp shirts and special treats.

The morning TV show interviewed Dr. Dale Geiger who is Director of the American Insti-

tute of Dog Behavior. Dr. Geiger claims to be a
dog psychologist with a new philosophy in dog
training, completely different from current
methods. He believes that learning must be
communicated to the dog by projecting men-
tally, not physically, to the dog. Restraint or
discipline should never be used on a dog. "If we
want a dog to lie down, we must create within
the dog a want to not stand up and not com-
mand the dog to obey." Dr. Geiger claimed his
institute has trained thousands of people, including movie stars, on how to have a har-
monious experience with their pets. According
to Geiger, if we transmit a feeling of generosity
and love to a dog, the dog reflects this back—
this is the principle of Allelomimetic Behavior.
The owner of a dog must recognize his responsibility to his dog and society, and behave in a
manner so that the dog's life reflects creditably
on both. The dog must be a member of the
household with equal rights and be a fully inte-
grated member of the family. If the dog detects
that it's unfairly and nonequally treated, it will
suffer trauma and display an opposition reflex.
Biting people, killing chickens, and chasing
motorcycles in the mind of the dog are ways of

expressing the opposition reflex. If the dog owner subconsciously rejects authority, the dog will attack mailmen and policemen, and if the dog owner dislikes hippies the dog will attack long-haired and slovenly dressed individuals. The tuition for the American Institute of Dog Behavior Course is $750 per session for owner and animal; however, there is a waiting list and there may be a six months delay before admission. Barf! Barf!

A special planning commission meeting tonight. Several township residents requested a discussion concerning a pack of wild dogs—the township police, the township dog officer, the township planning commission, and the township supervisors, seven residents, and the press. I am sure that the newspaper headlines tomorrow will have a medieval horror-story lead— "Savage Canine Pack Ravages Township Residents" or "Wolf-Dogs Terrorize Township— Officials at Loss of What Should Be Done." One of the residents reported that her son, while delivering papers, was chased by a dog. Several residents suggested that the dogs may chase deer and livestock; there is good reason for such concern. Yearly the department of agriculture in our state pays about $35,000 to farmers for sheep and other farm animals killed by dogs. The state conservation department reported 1,305 deer killed by dogs last year. On the other hand, these "wild" dogs seem to be safer than some "tame dogs." I know of one lady no one had better attack; she has a guard dog that kills upon command. She walks the animal on the streets as if it were a poodle or some other tame animal. I always fear that someday a two-year-old will run up to the "nice dog" and get torn apart. I can't help but hope that some night this lady will encounter a criminal with a "mugger dog." These dogs are trained to attack people and hold them while the master removes watches, rings, and wallets. There are also dogs that serve as matchmakers for gay guys and pimps for streetwalkers. I wonder how pimp dogs spend their time during layovers. It hardly seems proper for a dog to spend its time in a cathouse.

Dogs have the best press in the world. I suspect that there are between one and two million people bitten each year in the U.S. by "man's best friend." In addition, sixty-five or so diseases are transmitted from dogs to man; also ticks, fleas, and other pests are fostered by dogs to the detriment of man; sidewalks and lawns are made into fecal depositories. Each year in the U.S. dog-related spending amounts to about $700 million for purchase costs, $600 million for veterinary fees, $550 million for dog food, $300 million for licensing, $450 million for clothes and accessories, and $400 million for miscellaneous items, like superdooper pooper scoopers. The "muttiose" controls a considerable portion of the nation's wealth.

On the other hand, pigeons have a very bad press in the United States. There are so many bad jokes about pigeons that many people laugh at the mere mention of them. Similarly they laugh at the mention of prunes and dog catchers.

Most Europeans consider pigeons attractive urban birds. There is a wide variety. Variants of the feral pigeon may be blue, gray, black, silver, brown, red, or white; markings may be bars, spots, and streaks; often they have iridescence of purple and green. Pigeon lovers give names to these variants: blue, velvet, grizzle, black, red, powdered blue, stenciled, yellow bar, dun, silver, opal checker, bronze neck, and others. Propagated breeds, such as the English pouter, black nun, white king, and white runt, often escape the lofts of pigeon fanciers and add to the multiplicity of appearance of this bird. The voice of the feral pigeon is soft, varied, and appeasing. Flocks fly in close and striking patterns. Birds and people soon learn to recognize one another.

Pigeons mostly feed on garbage, spillage, and other human slobbage. In smaller towns and on the edges of cities, pigeons fly into the countryside to feed on grains and other wastage about farmyards. Pigeon farming offers an ideal way of scrounging without breaking the law. Pigeons can be faulted for their messiness and certain health and fire hazards associated with droppings and nests, but in contrast to dogs, pigeons are saintly. Even rats do more for man than dogs; most medical discoveries are tested on rats.

According to an item in a newspaper by a local veterinarian, more than 2,500 to 3,500 dogs and cats are born every hour, while there are 415 human births per hour. This means 22 to 30 million cats and dogs are born yearly in the United States for every 3½ million human births. The vet also said that even if he and all his fellow veterinarians worked full time at spaying cats and dogs, they could not stem the pet explosion.

Tonight's paper offers *"Snakes for Sale*, a wide variety, harmless and poisonous." Surprise your estranged spouse with a six-foot rattlesnake. Each year at Fountain Cove they hold a rattlesnake hunt. There is a festive, carnival-like atmosphere about the whole affair. There are prizes for the longest snake captured, the most snakes captured—by a man, by a woman, by a child. Old Doc Sanders entertains the crowds of onlookers by teasing, kicking, and biting the snakes. The crowds cheer vicious strikes by the snakes. The organizers of this show claim that the snakes are given to scientific institutions for research after the hunt; a friend of mine tried to obtain specimens in order to study the internal parasites of the snakes; he received no reply to his request. Each year six to ten people get bitten by rattlesnakes at the Fountain Cove Festival. Multiply this hunt by the other, similar ones in the United States and you can probably account for the majority of snakebite cases. I have spent many thousands of hours in the out-of-doors and the only two times I have seen rattlesnakes in the wild is when I have gone looking for them in their wintering dens. The only time I seriously hurt myself when in snake country was when I fell on a dead branch and injured my knee. I am sure that if all fallen branches and logs were removed from parks and other natural areas, they would be much safer, but less interesting. I object to snake-killing festivals, to pigeon shoots where thousands of birds are released for target practice, and the hunting of woodchucks just for the sport of killing. I do not object to the destruction of individuals or local populations of snakes, pigeons, woodchucks, or other animals when they represent a hazard to man or cause damage to man's crops or property. However, rattlesnakes, pigeons, and woodchucks play important roles in the scheme of nature, and their wanton destruction reduces the riches of a biological system.

I do not object to hunting by sportsmen; some of the greatest naturalists have been or are hunters. Unfortunately, not all hunters are sportsmen. The main event of hunting should be out-of-doors experience, not the killing of animals. The killing of the animals should represent a harvest of a surplus and the harvested animals should be utilized as food.

It is very difficult for most people to accept the reality that all relationships between man and an animal species have two sides. For every dog that picks out a skyjacker or detects a shipment of drugs, there are dogs that kill children or help to spread Rocky Mountain spotted fever to a suburban population.

Let us not forget the lady who wrote: "I have been a cat lover all of my life and I was very interested in the letter from your reader who wrote that she was uncertain about marriage to a medical student who had dissected a cat in his class work. Any person who would so treat a cat is not to be trusted. Such a person is invariably mean, vicious, and underhanded. Cats have a way of sensing such crimes as her fiancé has committed, and I believe the young lady would be wise to break the engagement with a person who does not share these feelings. Such marriages will fail. A cat hater should marry another cat hater—they deserve each other. The Egyptians were right, anyone who hates cats should be put to death." To such a cat lady, even old kittylitter smells nice.

I recently saw an ad in a comic book for children that really burned me. "Live Baby Squirrel Monkey, only $19.95. Send for one today. Be the happiest boy on your block. Have loads of fun and enjoyment. Train your monkey to do tricks." The ad pictured a monkey in striped pants. Each year, thousands of monkeys are sold to customers who have neither the knowledge nor the facilities for the proper care of simians; a large portion of these animals soon die or are disposed of because the owners did not realize what they were getting into. Those simians that are sold for pets represent only a small portion of about 200,000 live nonhuman primates that are traded each year. The major users of the simians are research laboratories. One major animal dealer in a thirty-eight-year period captured 1,250,000 small monkeys, 3,980 chimpanzees, 259 orangutans, and 198 gorillas; on these he grossed $28,600,000. Similarly, tropical birds and fishes are exploited.

Perhaps the worst villains of the pet world are those who place ads or erect roadside signs announcing free kittens, free cuddly puppies, or free ponies to someone who has a good home. Nothing creates more family strife than: "But Dad, why can't I have a free collie? I promise to take good care of it."

Wildlife now means different things to different segments of our population. To the ghetto dweller, the terms means rats, mice, bedbugs, lice, fleas, flies, cockroaches, and police dogs. Wildlife to the suburbanite may mean squirrels, starlings, sparrows, pigeons, mosquitoes, spiders, Japanese beetles; to this list he may add his pets—canaries, parakeets, cats, goldfish, and watch dogs. To many, animals are remote creatures kept behind bars or stuffed in museums or are nasty bugs to be Flitted or Raided.

Natural relationships between man and other animals have, once clearly recognized, become blurred and psychotic. For many, associations with animals have degraded into casual encounters—a cockroach running across the kitchen floor, a yearly visit to the zoo to show a child an elephant, a two dollar bet on the fifth race, feeding pigeons in the city park, or stepping over dog droppings on a sidewalk.

Several years ago, one of my friends told me that her three and four-year olds could tell the "good" animals from the "bad" animals. She proceeded to demonstrate by asking them: Are tigers "good" or "bad"? Are snakes "good" or "bad"? I pointed out and demonstrated that her intonation and facial expressions were the clues the children were using and that I could make snakes "good" and cows "bad" by reversing her intonations and facial expressions. Most people are similarly naive about usefulness and destructiveness of animals. Goodness or badness are relative, and based on mankind being dominant. Cows are "good" when they produce milk and "bad" when they break down a fence and destroy a grain field; snakes are "bad" when a poisonous species bites a person and "good" when they eat rats and mice. From the point of view of the deer is man "good" or "bad"?

Although my daughter might say otherwise, I do not hate dogs or cats, but rather believe that not enough thought goes into most pet selection. No natural forest has 500 to 1,000 wolves to the square mile. No natural bird population could withstand a prey-to-predator ratio as exists in our urban areas. Mechanical predators play an important role in the urban scheme; probably five to ten million dogs and cats get run over each year in the United States. Zoo animals are presently suffering from illnesses caused by urban air and urban noise. Coal miners once used canaries as pollution detectors; we need again to study the verdict of our animals' associates.

Urbanites tend to assign human feelings, emotions, and motives to animals; their animals are unlike the livestock I rear on my farm, the wildlife I encourage about my home, or the insects of my professional life. A dog today is not a canine with canine needs, but a hairy member of the family that barks. A number of psychologists and psychiatrists have suggested that part of man's feeling of alienation and lack of purpose stems from an estrangement from nature.

There seems to me to be a great difference in the attitudes of the rural and the city people, when it comes to everyday living. Most urbanites are insulated against realities a farmer must face each day. A disease can extinguish a valuable animal. Pests can destroy or greatly reduce yields of a crop. Rain can delay operations, ruin a crop at a critical stage, flood a field, or cause any number of catastrophes. Drought, wind, freezing conditions, hail, and hot weather are additional natural unaccountables. A farmer has many axes in his ceiling and oftentimes one comes loose. If his hay is ready to harvest, he must risk rain or wait. If he waits and it does not rain, he has made a bad judgment. If he cuts the hay and it gets rained on, he also has made a bad judgment. If the hay is harvested without being rained on, according to some of his neighbors, "he was lucky." By and large, a farmer must make a multitude of decisions relating to the management of living organisms. His decisions must be grounded in knowledge, effected by the uncertainty of nature, and cannot be rescinded. Thus, a farmer must develop a philosophy of environmental management.

The urban man is a banker, a highway engineer, an English teacher, a postal clerk, a printer, a television repairman—a specialist who respects other specialists. If an urbanite has a rat problem, he will generally call a pest-control specialist to do the job; a farmer normally will do it himself. Specialization makes urban living possible, but also may be a major cause of frustration when one sector fails to function. Incompetency, poor management, strikes, traffic jams, breakdown of equipment, and dishonest employees are some of the failures that contribute to our present urban predicament. A specialist generally is not trained to a holistic environmental philosophy.

Because of attitudinal differences based on experience and mores, the farmer sees an animal from a different point of view than does an urbanite. A 4-H Club member will spend many long hours caring for a market lamb, fitting it for show, training it to hold and best display itself to be judged at a fair. When it comes time for the lamb to be sold, the 4-Her may have a momentary qualm, which quickly passes. He knows that new lambs will be coming next spring and why lambs are produced. This does not mean that farmers are callous or that farm animals receive poor care. Generally, farm animals receive excellent care, because they are treated as animals and are provided with space, nutriment, and health care according to their species.

On the other hand, urban pets are often unwisely loved by their owners. At fashionable pet shops one can purchase mink stoles, sailor suits, Easter hats, cashmere sweaters, necklaces, and sunglasses for canines. Some dog owners spend as much as $600 to $800 per year to have their dogs walked. However, other dogs are locked up in apartments from 7:30 AM to 5:30 PM or longer without a place to urinate. In most cases the family pet is treated as a substitute for a person. Instead of a rich experience in which a family learns about nutrition, animal development, and behavior, most pet owners have a stagnated experience the greatest reward of which is a bored lick of the hand and a layer of animal hair on the couch.

Many parents believe that by living with animals and feeding, observing, and taking care of pets, children will acquire a sense of responsibility. However, most city children are not allowed to develop mature relationships with animals. This is because the parents do not understand what function the animals are to perform. Is the animal to serve as refuge from unpleasant conflicts with the parents? If this is the case, will the parents accept the child's attachment to this pet without resentment to the child or the pet? Is the pet to serve as an instrument for a child's biological education? If so, will the parent allow the child to witness mating, birth, death, and other phenomena of life? Will the parent require the pet to be disciplined or will overpermissive parents extend their laxity to the pet, thus reinforcing their lesson of immaturity? Also, is the pet really for a child or is it for the parents? A dog doesn't go bowling with the boys in the evenings and doesn't complain about spending all morning watching soap operas.

Isn't man's almost fanatical obsession with dogs, cats, and other pets an indication of a paucity of animal associates? A growing number of psychologists are prescribing the use of pets in psychotherapy. Instead of going to the local drugstore to have the pharmacist compound an antacid taken thrice daily, we may be told to pet our Irish setter before every meal and just before we go to bed. The pet-store operator may have to take a two-year college program so as to know when a patient needs an affectionate beagle rather than an adorable poodle. Our understanding or lack of understanding of man's need for animal associates has reached a low when a pet must be prescribed as an antidote. Would not an animalscaped urban environment that recognized man's need for animal associates be a possible cure?

To a degree the urban dweller has recognized that plants are an essential part of the urbanscape. Indeed, landscape architects, a nursery industry, and park and recreation departments are concerned with providing plant life in the city. However, in most cases urban plantings are design features—soil stabilizers, display specimens, dividers for different uses, and screening for unsightly structures. Very few urbanites treat plants as a living basis of a community that includes the physical environment, plants, animals, and human life.

City planners have been so burdened untangling traffic snarls that they have not dealt with the urban ecosystem. Landscape architects and landscapers are concerned with serving their prime clientele, the land developers; pleasing customers does not solve environmental problems. My purpose is to suggest that in our rapidly deteriorating urban environment we must make a place for animal life. Also, we must consider those animals we already have in the city; do we need to have dogs and cats, to the exclusion of every other form of life? Can we, by planning, eliminate or reduce pest problems? We need to animalscape our cities so that they become complete and healthy habitations for mature humans. A city capable of supporting a rich and abundant wildlife has the capacity to humanize. I suggest the paradox of animals humanizing man, and that an environment hostile to animals is also hostile to man.

The first ecological lesson I learned as a young entomologist was "to turn rocks and logs back over when I was collecting insects." This meant that when I or another entomologist was out collecting the following year, there would likely be another harvest of insects from the same site. Albert Schweitzer suggested "a reverence for life." However, this reverence must go beyond the living thing; it must respect the source of life. In the case of my insects, the rocks and logs provided a necessary element, and restoring the cover allowed life to continue beyond the occupants of any one instant.

Certainly urban and rural America has a

munificence of problems—not all biological—
including crime, drugs, inadequate housing,
garbage, rats, corruption, and exploitation of
minorities. But it is up to the biologist to get off
his sphincter and fight for biologically sound
planning. Biologists, like too many other scientists, are preoccupied with defending their research territory, parading their wisdom, and
forecasting doom; they prim and prance in the
face of disaster. When grant monies are available, they sell their souls to discover ap-
proaches and to publish disciplined essays on
trivia. The first thing a biologist must do is to
defend life; all else is secondary.

CHAPTER 8

It Is Dangerous to Dream

"In 1868, with help of undergraduate students, President Evan Montgomery of the State University constructed a house for his new bride and himself." I read this about ten years ago when I briefly studied the history of the State University; it struck me as really neat. First, the president of the University knew how to build a house; second, the students learned important skills by actually doing the work; and third it is difficult not to respect one another when you sweat together to build something worthwhile. When I was ten, I spent an entire day hoeing corn with my father for the first time; my blistered hands gave me new respect for him. The land-grant university system was founded on the concept of learning by doing. One can of course fault the present leadership of agriculture for moving away from this concept, but one cannot fault the system as it functioned in the 1930s.

The city is a complex organism. The diversity of it makes it an exhilarating place to visit and a stimulating and ofttimes provoking place to live and work. A city is: a delicatessen run by Tony Dicecco who yells at the students from the nearby high school for cutting classes—a fruit store with enormous oranges and apples and glorious grapes that ring the Pavlovian bell of the commuters rushing to catch the 5:18 to Woodbridge Park—a bus driver who screams at a confused visitor from out of town for putting too much money in the collection machine, but then by a complex system of juggling the fares of other riders, returns the visitor's 20¢ overpayment six stops later—a store window featuring a bathtub built for two and a barbershop where plants are grown in such profusion that you expect to hear the call of the jungle birds while you get your hair trimmed—a little grocery store where Frank Musser and his wife, Lee, bake Bauerbrot like in the "Old Country"—a little old lady who lives on a $150 a month pension and feeds pigeons each day beneath the statute of General Henry W.

Halleck—a movie house that runs twenty-four hours a day, has five customers for the 4:21 A.M. feature and has regular reruns of popcorn-feeding mice—a building inspector who visits a newly opened clothing store the week before Christmas and then hems and haws about code violations until he "finds an inexpensive sports jacket that is marked down."

The city is a million inspirational, creative, desolate, and degenerative scenes. The city has a sharp edge that cuts. There are so many art stores, liquor stores, pizza places, Laundromats, and people, that one more or less seemingly makes no difference. However, each of the stores or businesses is somebody's dream.

In 1935, the yields on our family farm were 34 bushels of corn per acre; oat yields were 43 bushels and hay production was about ¾ ton per acre; our cows each produced 120 to 140 pounds of butterfat per year, our sows averaged 4 pigs per litter reared, and our chickens each laid about 40 eggs per year. When I was seven and my brother five, father asked us what we would like to see. We thought about it a while and told father that we would like to see $100, all at one time. Father saved his monthly milk check, his check for the sale of ten 250-pound pigs, mother's egg money for the month, and the money from the sale of garden produce; this amounted to $97.35; by searching the entire house for stray pennies and other change, we were only able to expand the sum to $99.76. Nonetheless we believed that father was rich.

By 1948, our corn yields were 94 bushels, oats 115 bushels, and alfalfa hay more than 3 tons per acre; the cows averaged 485 pounds of butterfat, the sows averaged 9 pigs per litter, and the chickens each laid 200 eggs per year. Father bought a new tractor.

In the time that it took for me to grow from boy to man, rural life underwent a remarkable metamorphosis associated with agricultural research and extension. Our family was deeply involved in this movement. My father was a 4-H Club leader for twenty-five years and each of his three sons were club members. One year, his 4-H Club Dairy Judging Team ranked third in the United States. Like most teachers, father had to learn more than his students. I remember going to one 4-H Club meeting when I was six. Two members, 12 and 14, hired themselves out on Saturdays for a month previous to meeting night to earn enough money to paint one side of their old farmhouse, so that the movie to be shown at the 4-H meeting would have a white surface for the screen. Painting one side of their farmhouse was the first step taken by that family toward becoming one of the outstanding farm families in that county. Across rural America, mothers and fathers learned by teaching their sons and daughters. Today I have farmer friends who ski, play tennis, and vacation in Europe. The rustic with the straw hat and sprig of timothy in his mouth was slain by an extension specialist from the state university. Who has contributed most to America, the great men of the National Academy or the extension specialist of the 30s?

The agricultural teachers, the researchers, the rural leaders of the United States dared to dream of a country where the farmer could produce food and fiber in abundance and yet live in comfort and work with enlightenment. The heart of the movement was based on practical, technical educational leadership for the family and the community. The leadership was not imposed from the top, but came from and developed within the community. The technique of demonstration and of directly teaching individual farmers with their neighbors observing the results was highly effective. The prime factor of success was that the agricultural teachers and researchers of the 1930s had a vision.

One of my colleagues trains his wildlife-management students by placing a lead rope in their hands with an almost tame deer on the other end. The student is dragged about by the deer and learns on what plants the deer browses and how the deer spends its day. I suggest that similar training is necessary for city planners and architects. They need to follow a conventioneer bent on a wild night out, observe young lovers window shopping, ride with scrub women at 2:15 AM on the subway, and discover the functions and disfunctions, so that they can find the glue to put our cities together again. But most of all there must be a vision that will lift up the spirit of the urbanite so that he no longer considers the city a hopeless trap from which he must escape.

One lady with a plate of cookies does more to make a neighborhood than does a planning commission. I got this message on a Christmas card from one of my mother's former neighbors. My mother served as a catalyst for neighboring in the subdivision where she lived for the last eleven years of her life. The card noted how since mother's death the friendliness of the neighborhood seems to be disappearing. The cookie lady is gone. I fear that most planners don't really understand the art of neighboring. Tearing down fences isn't the answer; creating gates in the fences is what is required.

Grandmother Clark isn't really anybody's grandmother; her children and grandchildren have all moved away; but, she is everybody's grandmother. She is an eighty-one-year-old widow who lives in the little hamlet of Nutley. There are eighteen houses, one store, and a church at two country crossroads. Grandmother Clark has a large garden, keeps chickens in her backyard, and makes her famous chocolate doughnuts which are the manna of the local church suppers. Although she lives alone and has for twenty-two years, she has grandmothered almost all the adults and children in Nudley and on the nearby farms. She is a true neighbor and the most important person in Nudley.

Ben Hetrick died last Friday at age sixty-three; Ben really wasn't anybody. He lived off an alley in Beatty Lane, never held a job for more than six months, was mostly disagreeable, dirty, and drunk. Still, the residents of Beatty Lane raised money for his funeral, sent flowers, and a respectable number attended the services at the Beatty Lane Community Church. The simple reason was that Ben Hetrick was a neighbor.

Architects construct monuments to their own egos. Engineers design roads for cars. Developers have so many lots to an acre. Builders construct houses with one, two, three, or four bedrooms. Planners review pieces of paper. All forget that houses and cities are for people. It is important for Grandmother Morgan to live near her daughter and son-in-law, because Grandmother Morgan cannot drive a car and she likes to see her grandchildren, but she could not stand the strain of living in the same house with five active children between the ages of three and nine. Do architects, engineers, developers, builders, or planners address themselves to the real problems of Grandmother Morgan and her daughter? I fear that none do. Zoning ordinances do not allow houses to be subdivided or added to or allow mobile homes to be placed in R2 even if for only eight, or how many, years Grandmother Morgan has left. The most daring planning commission would be fearful of an innovative solution. R1, R2, R3, and R4 are sacred. The peas, the mashed potatoes, the pork chops on our plates must be safely separated from each other. R1 people must not associate with R3 people and Grandmother Morgan would be better off anyway living with other old people like herself in a "Golden Village."

When a neighborhood, on its own, decides to become healthy, even zoning boards, planning commissions, and elected officials cannot stop this from happening. Ten years ago, Beatty Lane was an acknowledged slum. Since then our planning commission has spent many hours discussing how by zoning or other means Beatty Lane could be upgraded. The zoning board allowed almost anything to get by, "because anything that happened in Beatty Lane was for the better." The supervisors passed a junk ordinance, a rodent-control ordinance, and half a dozen other ordinances so as to solve

Beatty Lane's problems. While the planners talked, the zoning board granted variances, and the supervisors enacted laws, the residents of Beatty Lane repaired houses, planted flowers, and built a new church. However, the educated residents of the region and the schools still give the ghetto treatment to people living on Beatty Lane; they still are "shat" upon. However, Beatty is no longer a physical slum; it may never have been a social slum, but in a strong university community anything that is blue-collar and a little redneck is granted inferior status. I think that Beatty Laners may no longer even be a psychological slum. For the first time last night, they attended a township meeting and "stood up for their rights." They opposed the construction of a multifamily unit near "their park." You've come a long way Beatty, with your little dreams.

I regularly observe the robustness of the community where my in-laws live. I note the success of certain businesses such as book stores, the kinds of crafts and art wares that are available, the numbers and kinds of restaurants, and what is happening to the businesses which are on the fringe of the commercial districts. The thing that strikes me most about urban businesses is the general lack of knowledge of their competition. When I ask one art dealer about another art dealer two blocks away, I find that he doesn't know anything about the other dealer's specialty. In fact, he has never even been in the other guy's store and thinks it is a frame shop. This kind of isolation passed from the agricultural scene twenty or more years ago. Mushroom growers talk to other mushroom growers and fruit producers talk to other fruit producers. The secret formula never was a secret. Farmer groups attend conferences and short courses planned by their state universities and their state associations; agricultural leaders gather to organize educational programs and establish research priorities.

I recently visited an urban community with a dream. The city was deeply committed to education. Each school was the center of community cultural life. The elementary schools were alive with adult and youth activities. On the day I visited one school, a Puerto Rican mothers' group was preparing a special luncheon for the teachers as an introduction to traditions of Puerto Rico. A group of hefty ladies were discussing sensible dieting in another room. The school dental technician was preparing the second-grade class for their yearly check-up (if the child came from a family which could not afford dental work, arrangements would be made for state agencies to cover the cost; if the family could not afford to pay dental work all at one time, a payment system was arranged between the dentist and the family; or if finance was not a problem, an appointment with the family dentist was arranged); it was impressive to see a dentist's office located in school. There was also an examining room so that prospective mothers could have their medical check-ups at the school. The home extension worker taught classes and produced a newsletter on nutrition at the school. A community swimming pool and a park were jointly shared by the school and the city recreation department; the programs of the school and of the recreation department complemented one another. That evening we returned to school to find fathers and sons building boats together, older people square dancing, a special course to help young parents to deal with child-rearing problems, and a dozen other activities. I was told that more than 70 percent of the adult residents of the community are involved in one or more of the school's programs.

During the several days that I spent in this city with a community-educational program, I also visited a high school and a vocational school. At the high school there was a special law program where students learned citizen-rights. Also, for those with special interest in this area, arrangements were made to spend time with police on patrol, visiting courtrooms, and meeting lawyers and judges. The state employment office was located in the high school.

At the technical school, I found that local employer's committees guided the instructors in what skills were to be taught, so that the most modern techniques were presented. The guidance departments at the schools had employment records for their graduates that were updated twice yearly; guidance staffs seemed honestly concerned about the individual achievements of each of their graduates; students were not just herded through and released after four years. Many graduates continued to take special courses at the schools to improve their employment opportunities. There were people of all ages and colors in the classes.

The city itself was involved in an international friendship program with another city by means of a kind of yearly Olympiad arrangement. Wherever I went in this city, everyone I saw had a kind of contagious enthusiasm and pride in themselves and in their community. I had found what the Dutch call *gezelligheid* living in an American city. The people of this community had a dream.

Such dreams are powerful stuff. Two white brothers and a peace-loving black brother had dreams for America and were shot for them. I wonder if it is still possible to find national leaders who are more than political hacks? I wonder if there are still educators who inspire greatness in young people? I wonder if there are still physicians who are more concerned with improving their skills in the operating room than on the golf green? I wonder if there are still businessmen who are more concerned with their customers' needs than with their dollars? I wonder if there is some Great Awarder who insures that wise political leaders, and inspiring teachers will succeed? Or is it that each person must start leading, must start teaching, must start being conscious, must start being honest, must start dreaming and caring?

If so, I will dream of a time when land is no longer merchandise, but has a bill of rights to protect it from exploitation, when cities are again centers of the higher arts and the good life, when builders understand the physical, biological, and artistic properties of their construction materials, when truck drivers own library cards, public meetings are well attended, and politicians are not all lawyers. Buildings will be designed by architectural firms that have consulting janitors, policemen, window washers, pest-control operators, and firemen on their staffs. Sidewalks will be poured with a slope, so that water from melting snow will run off, and biologists will help to design and plan cities.

Then some bright May morning my daughter's family will pack a picnic lunch and travel by bicycle to visit a field of yellow lady's slippers. Her family will not have to approach the field secretively for fear of exposing these flower

gems to ignoble plant collectors or other ig-
noramuses. The field of orchids will be protected from land developers, because all the
citizenry of the community will recognize that
a field of orchids is more valuable than thirty
home sites. No horse lover would dare canter
his mare here nor would a park director dream
of constructing a baseball field near this site.
Even the highway engineer dare not intrude,
because all of America is a community of lady's
slipper lovers.

Index

Agricultural extension movement, 162, 163

Amsterdam, 33, 93

Animal scaping suggested, 155

Automobile:
  caused problems, 45, 46, 47
  idolatry, 51, 52

Biologists, 130, 131, 132, 157, 164

Bureaucrats, 104, 105

Cats, 143, 146, 147, 148, 149, 156

Cities, vacations, 53-58

Cemetery planning, 113-122

Central Park, New York City, 88, 89

Charlatans, environmental, 60-63, 68

Community education, 169-171

Dogs, 135, 138-142, 143, 146, 148, 149, 150, 153, 154, 156

Diversity, lack of, 122, 123, 124, 125, 126, 127, 128, 129, 130, 132, 133

175

Dutch elm disease, 130
Ecosystem, complexity of, 125-129
Elm tree problems, 130
Environmental charlatans, 60-63, 68
Environmental philosophy, 151-152
Environmental Protection Agency, 110, 111
4-H club activities, 14, 16, 17, 152, 162-163
Garbage removal, 29
Governmental planning, 58, 59, 60
Government, special interest groups and, 72, 73-75,
    78-80, 86
Habitat improvement association suggested, 125
Highway-construction-related problems, 35-37, 41-44,
    94-95
Highway encroachment on agricultural lands, 12-15,
    39-40, 49-50
Housing, low-income, 95-97
Housing standards, 87, 102-103
Humanitarian considerations in planning, 71, 76-77,
    83-84, 106, 108-109, 164-172
Insects, importance in ecosystem, 125
Land development, 87
Laws versus education, 105-106
Medical services, 24-25
Motorcycle tracks, 50-51
Olmstead, Frederick, 88
Pedestrian versus the automobile, 47-49
Personal freedom, 106-108
Pests, 46, 149-151, 153

Pets, 147, 152-154

Pets, psychotherapy and, 154-155

Philosophy, environmental, 151-152

Phloem necrosis, 130

Pigeons, 90, 142-143, 145

Parks and open spaces, 90-94

Planners, circumventing them, 66-68, 99-101

Planning, humanitarian considerations, 71, 76-77, 83-84, 106, 108-109, 164-172

Schools, 17-18, 24, 169-171

Schweitzer, Albert, 156

Shade tree commission, 129

Snakes, 144-145, 149

Urban ecosystems, 155

Urban problems, 32-34, 168-169,

Urbanization of rural communities, 20, 23, 26-27

"Watering holes," 92-93

Weed control laws, 132-133

Weeds, importance of ecosystem, 125

Zoning, 85, 167

Index 177

URBS (cont.)
Water balance, spatial 154 ff
Pathways in watersheds 172
Urban... 60 ff
Urban pollution 164
Urban ecosystems 60 ff
Urban... budgets 65 ff 69 ff
... hydrology ... 60 ff
Water, the urban 60 ff
... balance 172 ff
Water flow system 154
Shade trees, cooling 61
Stormwater 140
Urban ecosystems 1
Urban heat island 2 60 60 ff
Urbanization of land resources 75 ff 74 ff
Water balance 64 65 ff
Watershed 63 65 ff
Management ... 36
Waterways 60